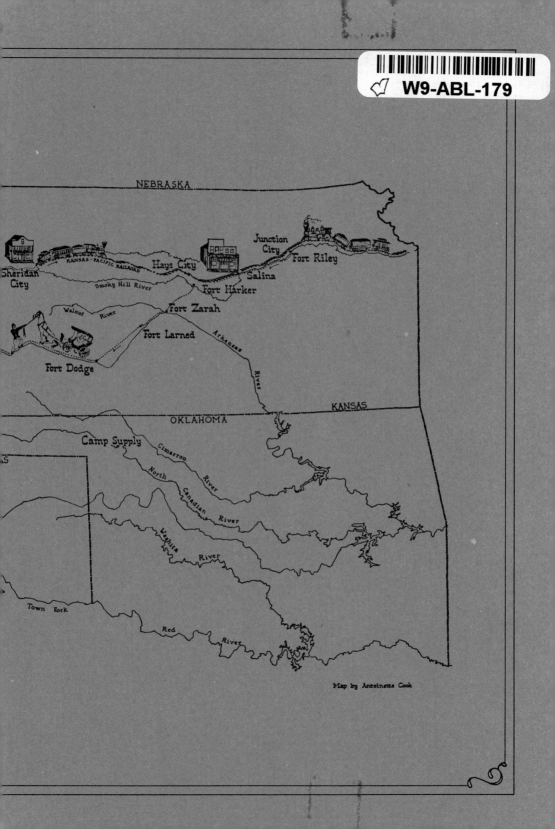

NEBRASKA

KANSAS · PACIFIC RAILROAD

Hays City

Junction City

Fort Riley

Sheridan City

Salina

Smoky Hill River

Fort Harker

Walnut River

Fort Zarah

Fort Larned

Arkansas River

Fort Dodge

KANSAS

OKLAHOMA

Camp Supply

Cimarron River

North Canadian River

Washita River

Town Fork

Red River

Map by Antoinette Cook

An Army Wife on the Frontier

Number Six of the Series

UTAH, THE MORMONS, AND THE WEST

The purpose of this series is
to make available both unpublished manuscripts
and others that are now out of print.
Selection is based upon
their intellectual appeal as accurate history
and their emotional interest
as good literature.

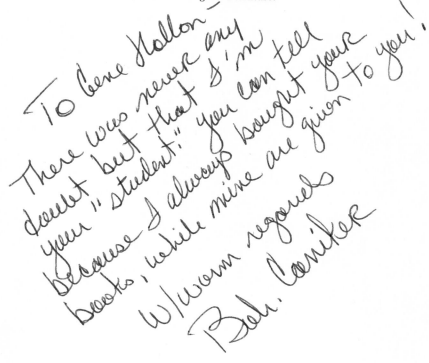

To Gene Hollon —
There was never any
doubt but that I'm
your "student!" You can tell
because I always bought your
books, while mine are given to you!
w/warm regards
Bob Carriker

Lieutenant Frank D. Baldwin and his bride, Alice Blackwood,
January 1867.

An Army Wife on the Frontier

THE MEMOIRS OF ALICE BLACKWOOD BALDWIN
1867–1877

Edited and with an Introduction by

Robert C. and Eleanor R. Carriker

Published by Tanner Trust Fund
University of Utah Library
Salt Lake City, Utah

Contents

Illustrations

Introduction

Life in the Indian-fighting army was harder on wives than husbands. The frail young woman from "back East," whisked to the Indian-active West by a knight errant in officer's dress, often found her duties much more than those of an ordinary helpmate. The regular household and wifely tasks were performed, but frequently under unusual and trying circumstances. Years of anxiety took their toll. Childbearing was dangerous and unattended, while family life suffered from a too often absent husband. Housing accommodations at frontier posts were shabby at best, if officers' quarters were even available. Indian attacks were always a potential threat, though the ever-present insects, snakes, and rodents were a more realistic fear. In far too short a time the bride's age was no longer accurately reflected in her wrinkled face. Clearly, the army wife earned her husband's promotions as much as he.

Though much is known about the exploits of the Indian-fighting officers of the army, less is known of their wives than any other group of frontier females. Numerous books elucidate the importance of William T. Sherman, Nelson A. Miles, George Crook, and dozens of others, but almost nowhere is there a companion volume on the officer's spouse. Partially this oversight has been due to a lack of interest in women's studies, a situation now happily remedied, and partially it was due to the paucity of published and unpublished material available on women who made their homes in the more than one hundred military camps of the Indian-wars West.

The memoirs and personal correspondence of Alice Blackwood Baldwin are, fortunately, present and accounted for. They are vibrant remembrances by an articulate woman who lived an interesting life. In 1874 Alice instructed her husband, "Frank I wish you would burn up all my letters to you after you read them because I have written in most every one something I wouldn't want anyone else to see and if anything should happen to you then [they] would fall in someones hands — so be sure and destroy them." [1] Contrary to Alice's wishes, Frank Baldwin did not destroy his wife's correspondence. Some 327 letters remain today in the custody of the Henry E. Huntington Library, and, together with the memoirs written about 1917 and first published in 1929, they offer the reader a most incisive experience into the behavior of the frontier army wife.

The pioneer spirit was early cultivated in Alice Blackwood. Born in Ann Arbor, Michigan, of transplanted New York parents, she moved with her family to the Far West gold fields by overland wagon train in 1854 and settled at Sacramento. Two years later the mother passed on and Alice and a sister returned to Michigan. Residence was made with a childless aunt and uncle in Northville until it was time to enroll in the Albion Female Seminary. The father, meantime, died in California without ever having returned East to see his daughters.

It was a lonely childhood Alice suffered and the boarding seminary seemed more home than school. Among her class-

---

[1] Alice Baldwin to Frank Baldwin, September 15, 1874. All correspondence cited is in the Frank D. Baldwin Collection, Henry E. Huntington Library, San Marino, California.

mates were Rowena and Gertrude Baldwin from Constantine, Michigan. In May 1863 Alice was introduced to her friends' older brother Frank, a recuperating captain of the Nineteenth Michigan Volunteer Infantry recently paroled from Libby Prison, Virginia, in exchange for Confederate captives. Frank would return to active duty shortly, but the acquaintance begun with Alice blossomed into courtship and eventually marriage four years later.

The bridegroom at the January 1867 ceremony uniting Frank and Alice was a dashing figure. Entering the Civil War as a nineteen-year-old second lieutenant, Baldwin rose quickly through the ranks until he was mustered out four years later as a lieutenant colonel. During his tenure with the Nineteenth Michigan Infantry, Baldwin experienced no fewer than seventeen engagements, was twice taken prisoner, and served his command so courageously in Sherman's March to Atlanta he was later awarded the Congressional Medal of Honor.

After a brief, unsatisfactory experience farming and attending Hillsdale College in his native Michigan, young Baldwin accepted an appointment in February 1866 as second lieutenant in the regular army unit of the Nineteenth Infantry. It was a fateful decision, for the military became his lifelong career. The service was to Baldwin's liking and especially so when his battalion was ordered to Kansas where it guarded the stage routes between Forts Harker and Ellsworth. The isolation of the Kansas prairies moved Baldwin to great loneliness and in an impulsive moment he proposed to Alice by mail and rushed to her side before the close of the year.

Following a church wedding in Northville, the happy couple spent a week visiting relatives and then set out by train for their new home at Fort Harker. Surviving inclement weather and inadequate accommodations, the honeymooners successfully arrived and established themselves at the post. Here Alice, accustomed to the pleasures of a finishing school, was shocked and dismayed at the inconvenience of frontier life. But Alice had great resiliency and with spunk and determination found that no frustration was unconquerable. In fact, she survived with grace and good humor her initiation into the fraternity later known as the Old Army.

In September of 1867 Baldwin's outfit was transferred to New Mexico Territory. Alice, now nearing her ninth month in Kansas was also in her eighth month of pregnancy. Fortunately the pace set by the command as it moved across Kansas and Colorado was liesurely for Alice incurred no complications from the trip. Everything went well until the command passed through Trinidad, Colorado Territory. Here Alice felt her time was at hand and gave birth on October 12 to a baby girl, Juanita Mary. In a few weeks she was able to continue on to Fort Union and then Fort Wingate where she rejoined her husband.

Alice certainly proved her tenacity that first year. She could hardly be referred to as a tenderfoot any more. The fates, it seemed, would surely recognize her courage and ease the course of her life. Such was not the case however. Not because the fates decreed an especially exhausting life for Alice Baldwin. Rather Alice was living only an ordinary life as the wife of an officer-husband in the West. Throughout the West hundreds of other army wives endured similar hardships.

After spending more than a year in New Mexico, Alice entered a new phase of wifely service: separation from her husband. Wives were ordered out of New Mexico Territory and Alice chose to return to Michigan with her child. Unlike today, getting there was not half the fun. The return trip tested Alice's nerve several times as she and her baby traveled roughly one thousand miles by stagecoach to Sheridan, Kansas, where they had an equal distance by rail to Northville.

ALICE'S DESPONDENT YEARS, 1869–1876

The events between Alice's journey East in 1869 and Frank's assignment to the Sioux War in 1876 are curiously omitted in the *Memoirs*. It is possible Alice did not wish to reenact with pen and memory the depression she suffered in that period. More probably those years are deleted because Alice had a remarkably positive attitude in later years and wished to emphasize to others only the humorous or little known events of her experiences. Whatever the reason, Alice learned two important lessons during this first forced separation: one was that a return to Michigan is not the same thing as a return "home"; the other was proficiency in the wifely technique of reluctant consent.

Upon her arrival at Uncle Robert Blackwood's home Alice was warmly welcomed. Days became weeks and before long tempers shortened. Frank's army pay was pitifully small and was needed to maintain himself in New Mexico leaving little to nothing for his wife and child. Alice and Nita, as she was called, were forced to live at the mercy of relatives. This naturally trying situation was further complicated by the fact that Alice, who had been reared by a modestly wealthy uncle, had married only a junior officer, and he, moreover, had an annoying habit of seeking loans from his wife's former guardian. Letter after letter from this period dramatizes the uneasiness within the Robert Blackwood home.

Alice also refined in this period of separation her womanly technique of negative approval or reluctant consent. In 1869 the army was reorganized. During the shake-up Frank announced to his wife a desire to transfer out of the Fifth Infantry, to which he was then assigned, and into the Seventh Cavalry. Alice responded with these two comments. The first communication, on August 15, read:

> Now I suppose you have been wondering when I am going to say something about your transferring in the cavalry. You know, my darling Frank, I do not stand in your way of promotion or other good advantages. But I am afraid if you get into the cavalry you will get killed quicker than in the infantry and if you should by my advising you . . . I should feel like a murderer all my life. . . . You are so anxious to get into that branch of service I want you to be satisfied. If you can work it out,

and want to be transferred I will consent. But I hate to.
After all, I want to do what is for your interest.

Two days later Alice followed with this comment: "My darling,
do as you see best about transferring into that cavalry. I want
you to do well and be prosperous like General Custer . . . ." [2]
Baldwin withdrew his application for transfer.

Some weeks following this exchange of letters Alice was able
to return to Frank's side as he was transferred to Fort Hays
where wives were allowed. Life was no less difficult for Alice
than her first year in the field, but a great deal more pleasurable
now that she was with her husband. If there was a lesson Alice
learned at this point it was that a wife must seek her husband's
promotions as urgently as he. Accordingly, Alice joined the
affairs of the post gentry, cultivated friendships with senior
officers' wives, and carefully studied the social as well as military
chain of command.

Keeping up a good social front was extremely difficult for a
junior officer's wife. A nurse for Nita was considered mandatory
for a good appearance and a woman was promptly hired at fifty
cents per week. But after two weeks, doctor bills resulting from
Nita's bad case of worms and a dentist bill for Alice necessitated
letting the nurse go. Alice paid her by giving her "a jacket I had
before I was married and a pair of drawers." Interestingly, the
same day she discharged the nurse Alice petitioned Frank for
another status symbol, $200.00 worth of Brussels carpet for their
home.[3] Meantime, Frank, too, was ambitious beyond his pay
and borrowed $1,000 from Uncle Robert to speculate in Kansas
farmland.

The Kansas land turned out to be a slow moving investment
and in the fall of 1870 Alice was sent back to Michigan so that
Frank could save the money to repay Uncle Robert. The second
"tour" of duty in Michigan was as unpleasant as the first, and
Alice petitioned Frank to sell the land "if you can get just

[2] Alice Baldwin to Frank Baldwin, August 15 and 17, 1869.

[3] Alice Baldwin to Frank Baldwin, October 13, 1869.

enough to pay up our debts. I am sick and soul sick of being eternally in debt. It is the greatest trouble of my life." A month later she followed with the admonition, ". . . sell that land for the price we gave for it if you can't do any better and pay-up your debt. Rather and better do that than have the cursed debt be the means of our living separate any longer. I can't endure such a life much longer." [4]

But Frank refused to sell the land and Alice remained at the mercy of others. "It mortifies me more than I can tell you," wrote Alice, "to see myself and child going from one place to another eating other people's food and intruding into other people's family circles." [5]

Even when Frank was transferred to recruiting duty in Detroit during 1873, Alice and Nita had no permanent home. What should have been a blessing to the native Michigan couple continued to be a burden. The Kansas land was now sold but at such a loss that Uncle Robert could not be repaid without further sacrifice by Alice. So for the fourth year Alice made the rounds of relatives in Coldwater, Northville, Constantine, and elsewhere.

Frank no less than Alice was gravely concerned over their financial dilemma and considered reentering the lightning rod business, a sideline he had pursued with great success prior to his marriage. Alice accurately summed up their threefold problems of money, status, and separation when she responded:

> Tho your project of entering into the business of selling lightning rods may be a good one do you think you can do so without detriment (however slight) to your profession? No matter if you are so poor as a rat appearances in the Army have got to be preserved and so far from observation and knowledge I find an officer cannot enlist into any traffic without disparagement to his pro-

[4] Alice Baldwin to Frank Baldwin, December 3, 1870, and January 20, 1871.

[5] Alice Baldwin to Frank Baldwin, January 19, 1871.

fession or rank. . . . I wish sometimes you were out of the
Army. If you could have a chance of making money, for
you never earn where you are. You say if I could be
satisfied with what I have I would be much happier. I
know that as well as you and I have tried to be but very
little succeeded. Mercy knows I would be contented
with a very little. As matters are I wish I was out on the
Plains again, remote from civilization or "Society" and
then I could go dressed in calico. Our purse is not ade-
quate for our station.

   I had fixed on the first day of July to go to Grand
Rapids. I have decided to stay there one week and then
go to Dan's, spend another week and then go home to
Detroit. Will you be able by that time to pay Uncle
Robert part of the $1,000 you borrowed to buy some
land in Kansas last year? If not I will prolong my stay
so as to give you a chance to save more. I have visited
out and am tired out. So near home and yet living
around.[6]

The pressure of the situation forced Alice into an important
decision. Frank must win promotion or leave the service. No
deadline was set, but correspondence between the two makes it
clear Alice would not wait too much longer for results. To
achieve promotion Alice embarked on a program of quiet tea-
party politics by herself and hopeful newspaper exposure by her
husband.

In mid-1874 Frank was selected chief of scouts for Colonel
Nelson A. Miles's Indian Territory Expedition in the Red River
War against hostile Cheyennes. Here was the opportunity Alice
sought. Publicity was necessary for promotion in the post-Civil
War army and Alice realized that great profit was potentially
theirs if Frank would keep a diary of his experiences against the
Indians. Baldwin had kept a shirt-pocket size diary during the
Civil War, but for Alice that was not enough. What if it should
be lost? To guard against such a possibility Alice required her
husband to keep a second, more comprehensive, journal when-

   [6] Alice Baldwin to Frank Baldwin, January 24, 1873.

ever a relaxation in tempo permitted. To a degree this clashed with Baldwin's will and he wrote her:

> I am keeping a diary and probably should do as you suggest. You know, my darling, that I write all I can but that is all and I shall do all that I can to gratify your feelings of ambition which is no less than my own. But remember that glory in my profession is won only in battle, though men may and will add to it by skillful use of words.

A dozen days later he added:

> As you proposed I have got a large book in which I propose to keep a complete record of my movements from the day I left Newport [Kentucky] and when we get through I will turn it over to my little wife who is the most competent person I know of to enlarge and embellish it, etc.[7]

Alice was correct in her presumption that Frank would distinguish himself in this campaign. Baldwin participated in four serious engagements with the Indians, one of which, a rescue of two white girls from the Cheyenne earned him a second Congressional Medal of Honor. When the war was concluded Alice wrote up some excerpts from Frank's diary and submitted them to Colonel Richard Dodge, well-known author of frontier experiences. He summarily rejected the manuscript. This infuriated Alice as she had hoped for big things. "That was an awful disappointment to me, and I had counted so much on it. I will never get over it, I don't believe."

The conclusion of the Red River War in 1875 saw Frank stationed at Fort Leavenworth, Kansas — without a change in rank. Alice was visibly unhappy about the fact and laid the blame squarely on Colonel Miles. She felt Miles had taken advantage of Frank's tenacity during the Indian Territory Expedition and now was slow in recommending promotion.

---

[7] Frank Baldwin to Alice Baldwin, September 12 and 24, 1874.

Throughout the campaign Alice had complained of the hardships Miles forced on Frank in letters such as this:

> . . . it seems to me as if Miles was making you do all the drudgery of the whole command. Why don't he hazzard someone else's life besides yours. The other officers are left safe and unharmed. I wish Miles was dead or something. He ought to think of me away here, so anxious I am half dead. No one thinks of me. I have to think for myself and have had lots of trouble, too.[8]

When George Custer published his book *My Life on the Plains* in 1874, concurrent with Alice's manuscript rejection by Dodge, the pestering became more intense. Actually, Miles regarded Baldwin highly not only as a courageous soldier, but also as a trusted friend. If promotions were his to give he would do so, but, unfortunately, in spite of the recent successful campaign his outspokenness against General John Pope and others actually placed his own career in jeopardy. Frank, for his part, loved the army and was content with a warm personal relationship with Miles. Alice felt betrayed.

Outraged that neither promotion nor publicity resulted from Frank's term as chief of scouts, Alice badgered Frank into a promise that in future campaigns he would not accept hazardous duty assignments. When the Fifth Infantry under Miles suddenly entered the Sioux War following the Custer disaster, Frank carried this oath to the Northern Plains and was faithful to it as he wrote Alice:

> Where they talk [of volunteering] I lay back and keep my mouth shut, and I have expressed myself fully about being sent off on trips like that scouts should go on and I have said I would not go on any such rides as I have made, that I would resign before I would go and so I will . . . . While I will do my duty to the Government, I will do no more.[9]

[8] Alice Baldwin to Frank Baldwin, October 27, 1874.

[9] Frank Baldwin to Alice Baldwin, August 4, 1876.

But Frank was a soldier, a fighter, and a man. Before long he broke his promise and distinguished himself in three battles with the Sioux. Ironically, Frank's much publicized attacks against Sitting Bull brought him the newspaper attention and long-deserved military recognition he needed to win promotion to the rank of captain.

Recommendation for promotion — the first in ten years of service — could not stem the resentment Alice continued to harbor against the army. Increasingly her letters took on a despondent tone. Normal as her reaction may have been to a decade of official frustration, social slights, and long periods of separation from her husband, Alice's conduct was detrimental to her husband.

In one case, during November 1876, Frank had just made a tedious month-long train and steamer trip down and back up the Missouri and Yellowstone rivers. He sat in camp on the far eastern edge of Montana, physically exhausted, mentally questioning the capacity of his troops to combat the Sioux, and freezing in thirty-eight degrees below zero cold. His first letter from Alice in a month read:

> I have a headache this morning. I went to a concert given by a German military band which was very fine. ... I intend to accept every invitation I get this winter to places of amusement and enjoy them while I can, for that is the only time when I do always enjoy myself. I have none at home — I live so plain and quiet and have such dismal prospects in store I am unhappy as I can be sometimes. I try to overcome it but I can't always. Others here are no better than I but better off. I don't believe there is a single thing in connection with me or mine that anyone envies. ... I feel that I shall be buried in oblivion and had an unhappy, longing life. I see no other light .... I wish I could send you something for Christmas but I will have no money, I fear. Well, Frank, good-bye. May the Lord protect you is the best wish I can utter — and I don't have much faith in him. (signed) Your true loving wife.[10]

[10] Alice Baldwin to Frank Baldwin, November 5, 1876.

Similar correspondence was directed north from Fort Leavenworth all that winter. When the restriction against wives in the combat zone was relaxed in the spring of 1877, Frank urged Alice to join him at Fort Keogh. Caught between a wish to avoid all that living in a frontier post entails, and yet knowing her responsibility toward her husband, Alice made plans to ascend the Missouri. Alice's letters to Frank more accurately reflect her emotions at this decision than the lightheartedness portrayed in the *Memoirs*. One note offered these comments:

> As the time draws near for my banishment from this world I feel melancholy and depressed. I have got to go to a new and wild country full of foes and dangers. I am not prepared to live as I know I shall be obliged and you to be away from me in all probabilities. I shall see nothing cheerful or bright in the prospect. I shall always think as I do now that the sooner you get out of the 5th US [Infantry] the better it will be for you.[11]

Life at Fort Keogh was filled with tension for Alice. This time, unlike the Red River War, Alice was within the circle of hostilities. And as predicted earlier Frank was away from the post for long periods at a stretch. Rumors daily told of one or another disaster and it took a strong woman not to bend under the strain.

THE BALDWINS AFTER 1877

Regretably, Alice closes her memoirs at 1877. This is truly sad because the turning point in Frank's life was the Sioux War. From here on life would be much improved for the couple.

Recognition of Baldwin's leadership abilities by the press and his superiors was, oddly, not the most important development in a series of events that improved his career. The crucial event was Frank's declining state of health. Four consecutive winters in the unyielding Yellowstone country and eleven out of the past twelve years in frontier posts had taken their toll.

---

[11] Alice Baldwin to Frank Baldwin, April 14, 1877.

An illness he passed off for years as whooping cough was diag-
nosed late in 1878 as an active tubercular condition of the
right lung.

Interestingly, the same army that Alice and Frank felt had
neglected them for a decade or more suddenly showed great
interest in the thirty-six-year-old officer. Special arrangements
were made for the Baldwins to spend the remainder of the
1878–79 winter in Fort Augustine, Florida. When recovery
seemed certain Baldwin returned to Montana, but just as
quickly a relapse occurred. This time, by virtue of the direct
intervention of General Miles, Baldwin was assigned in 1880
as the American representative to several European military
conferences and was able to spend a good part of the next
winter in the south of France. Alice accompanied her husband,
perhaps because she had had so many frontier assignments she
demanded to share in this plush one; or perhaps it was because
she had become, over the years, a fast friend of Miles's wife and
felt partly responsible for maneuvering this great opportunity.
Juanita was safely tucked away at the Sacred Heart boarding
school in Detroit and Frank and Alice enjoyed their Grand
Tour.

Following the European trip Frank rose through a succes-
sion of new positions and promotions. For some unexplained
reason Baldwin was a rising star. Not that he became a powerful figure in the army, but he did occupy positions of importance
as judge advocate for the Department of the Pacific, Miles's
personal inspector at the Battle of Wounded Knee, and Indian
agent for the Kiowa and Comanche tribes of Oklahoma. His
rank rose to major.

Alice now seemed to enjoy the army. Pay was better, privileges more numerous, and most important was the fact that
after 1880 Frank was not stationed at remote posts in the colder
climes. When Baldwin was placed at a frontier post for a short
period, the general level of civilization was noticeably higher
than twenty years previous when Alice first started out, and
Alice especially reveled in the respect Frank held as either post

commander or ranking officer. So confident was Alice now that in 1894 when Frank Baldwin took his station as agent for the Kiowa and Comanche tribes in Oklahoma Territory, Alice listed some requirements before she would join her husband:

1. Must have a cat. Tom preferred.
2. W. C. [water closet] in the house or earth closet.
3. Good man servant about the shack, and, as you say, "plenty of help" in them.
4. Good stove as can be obtained to cook on.
5. Secure fastenings on doors.[12]

Frank Baldwin followed the Spanish-American War into the twentieth century, a rise in rank to colonel, and distinguished participation in the Philippine Insurrection. He retired to Denver in 1906 as a major general. Alice, meantime, tried her hand at short story writing, but without much encouragement from publishers.

Through all the years from her husband's junior officer status to retirement, Alice had, of course, changed. One desire that remained unaltered, however, was the one to publicize Frank's adventures. Accordingly, the same Alice who had required her husband to keep two diaries in 1874 (a practice Baldwin kept in fits and starts for the rest of his life) now helped him begin an autobiography forty years later. Frank's heart was in the project, but at this stage of his life he could not concentrate and the manuscript was never completed. A brief return to uniform as adjutant general of the State of Colorado during World War I served as a worthy excuse not to continue writing, and the old warrior never regained what little momentum he had had earlier.

The general passed away in 1923 and Alice brought together all his papers she could find. Incredibly, the handwritten autobiography plus the numerous diaries could not be located. Perhaps they were purposely secreted by an old man not anxious

[12] Alice Baldwin to Frank Baldwin, December 2, 1897.

to return to writing chores. Alice, who fancied herself an author of sorts following a few successes at writing historical features for local newspapers, was undeterred and began to edit a book with what material she had. Excerpts from official reports and a few previously published articles by men who had known Frank formed approximately a hundred pages of the proposed book. Since this clearly was not substantive enough, Alice contributed a like number of pages of her own memoirs that she had originally prepared as a separate book tentatively titled "Tales of the Old Army by an Old Army Girl." The final book was published in 1929 as *The Memoirs of the Late Major General Frank D. Baldwin,* though it was not truly reminiscences. In fact, the only true memoirs were those of Alice that made up the final and most interesting part of the whole volume.

It is Alice's section of the *Memoirs* that is here republished in a new edition with footnotes and map. Little has been done to alter the original printing save the corrections of the original publication's typographical errors, the additions of proper first or last names where called for, corrections of a few officers' ranks, and regularization of some army unit spellings. The *Memoirs* enjoyed only a modest sale before a fire in the publisher's warehouse limited distribution. The book today is very rare and valued at $75.00 when located.

Barely a year after the *Memoirs* came out Alice and Juanita, now the widow Mrs. A. C. G. Williams-Foote with four children, found Frank's missing autobiography. It was of little use now that the *Memoirs* were published, but the diaries and other papers were another matter. Alice and Juanita decided to sell piecemeal the entire collection of Frank's diaries, writings, maps, and correspondence. Times were hard in the 1930s for the family of six, now living in Santa Monica, California, as army benefits were meager. The decision to dispose of her husband's papers was not necessarily a gloomy one for Alice as she looked upon the sale as money to keep the family together, and also as a back door method to spread far and wide the adventures of Frank. She would yet give him the publicity he deserved even if it be only in private collections.

When Alice passed away in the early 1930s, Juanita continued to offer her father's things for sale to book dealers, newspapers, the Library of Congress, the Army War College, the Colorado Historical Society, and various universities including Montana and Harvard. Fortunately for history sales were exceedingly poor, and the collection remained relatively intact. Alice's own papers were added to the collection but they seemed even less valuable to buyers than Frank's material. In 1941, her perseverence waning, Juanita presented three thousand pieces of her father's papers, including the six hundred page handwritten autobiography, to the Henry E. Huntington Library of San Marino, California.

The bulk of the Frank Dwight Baldwin Collection in the Huntington Library concerned the affairs of Frank not Alice, though much of his correspondence to her was included. But in 1969 another cache of Baldwin material surfaced, and in addition to Frank's diaries there were several hundred letters pertaining to Alice plus some of her published and unpublished short stories.

Frank and Alice Baldwin were both remarkable persons. One was a double winner of the Congressional Medal of Honor, a courageous campaigner, and dedicated soldier. The other was an intelligent and spunky woman, equally dedicated to the Old Army. Singly or together, the Baldwins offer much insight into the frontier army. But of the two, Alice gives more information and anecdote from a seldom heard corner — the reluctant campaigner, the woman who waits at home.

My Ancestry—
Crossing the Plains

I was born in 1845, in Ann Arbor, Michigan, of good New England stock. My maternal grandfather served in the War of 1812. My father, Dr. Thomas Blackwood, was a native of New York, as was also my mother, who was Miss Jane Osborne. Their immediate ancestors, hailing from the New England states, were an extraction of Scotch, English and Irish. As my grandfather humorously remarked, in speaking of the family tree, "Not being descended from a long, unbroken line of noble ancestry of belted earls and knights of high degree," inasmuch as the blood of various nations flowed in our veins.

In religion, as a family, they were of the Presbyterian faith, firm and abiding characteristics of the staunch New Englanders, even leaning in their adherence to the stern and unyielding Covenanters, who regarded "letter writing on the Sabbath Day as sinful," the Sabbath beginning Saturday night and closing Sunday night at sundown. My mother being in delicate health, my father, who was a physician of repute, concluded a change of climate might be beneficial, and decided to remove to California, and further, to make the journey overland — a long, tedious and perilous one in those days, but most conducive to restoring health.

After much necessary preparation we started, traveling by railroad to St. Louis. The members of our party consisted of father, mother, my sister, Mary, later Mrs. M. T. Wallin, and myself. My mother's colored maid, Louisa, accompanied us. This was in 1854.

From St. Louis we took passage on the steamer, "Creole Belle," up the Missouri River, for Council Bluffs.[1] The trip was pleasant and uneventful, the boat being crowded with passengers, most of whom, like ourselves, were bound for the Golden West, some being invalids, others seeking their fortunes.

The broad and turbid waters of the Missouri were full of snags, and occasionally a sandbar would delay the boat, which did not improve the tempers of the voyagers. At such times, the negro crew and the firemen, with much profanity and "ye-ho-heaving," would gradually work the boat off the obstruction into open water, and the trip would be resumed.

Arriving at Council Bluffs, we disembarked, this being the starting point for all travellers and emigrants bound overland for the great, and comparatively unknown, trackless Plains.

A week or more was consumed in outfitting with all necessary conveniences for the long trip that would last for months — slow at best, even if no casualties occurred. Wagons with canvas covers were provided, one being fitted up especially comfortable for the ailing mother, with extending seats and straps suspended to the bed from the top of the wagon to ease, as much as possible, the rough roads to be encountered. In the commodious bed of the wagon was room for a rocking chair.[2]

[1] Council Bluffs was on the Iowa side of the Missouri River opposite present-day Omaha. The site was well known as the starting point for the Mormon Trail to the West.

[2] The Conestoga wagon, commonly called a prairie schooner, was three feet ten inches wide and twelve feet long at the bottom, but flared to sixteen feet long at the top.

Other wagons carried provisions and implements for the use of the employees who were to go along as hired help, escorts, etc.

There were many other wagon-trains in Council Bluffs, all bound for the West. To insure safety, and bearing in mind that there was "safety in numbers," the various trains joined forces, all drawn by the tie of mutual interest, and all having a kindly feeling toward each other and desiring to provide for and protect the women and children as much as possible.

Our wagons were drawn by oxen which, if not of lightning speed, were slow and sure. At night the wagons would camp in proximity to each other and be formed into a circle. Guards and sentries would be posted, and the travelers would gather around a huge bonfire and exchange social civilities and courtesies, or speculate on the journey's outcome and the prospects ahead of us. Some predicted danger and disaster; others, more optimistic, would enliven and cheer the darkening scene with song and music. There were some fine voices among our party which, accompanied by violin and guitar or accordion, diverted homesickness and sadness.

Among the singers was a young man named Robinson, unobtrusive and seldom joining in the mirth and conversation, who would sing in a clear and beautiful voice, "The Carrier Dove." This song, echoing among the hills and over the widening prairies, made a deep impression on me that will never be forgotten. I have often wondered if there are any survivors of our party who may remember this melancholy minstrel. Many warm friendships were made during our journey, and the monotony was not devoid of excitement and anxiety. Frequently herds of buffalo were seen in the distance, which incited the younger men of the party to leave the train and hunt the shaggy beasts. Rattlesnakes were numerous, as well as the ever-present prairie dog. The villages of the latter were often miles in extent, the little animals squeaking and barking at us as we passed. Many varieties of rabbits also were seen. Coyotes were numerous, although seldom seen during the day, but at night their melancholy howling was dismal and blood-curdling.

We came near having a tragedy in our train. In crossing a
stream, one of the employees of the train was caught in the
quicksand. He had gone on ahead to the stream to take a bath.
Plunging into the water, he felt himself being drawn down in
the treacherous mire. He shouted for help, which fortunately
was near, and a rope was thrown to him. This he fastened over
his shoulders and he was hauled ashore, greatly frightened and
exhausted, although none the worse for his adventure.

During the long journey the passing scenery was often
extraordinary and grotesque in the formations of rock and sand-
stone, at times resembling castles and parapets, domes and
towers and turrets, or pinnacles reaching high into the heavens.
Chimney Rock, a noted landmark on the Overland Trail, was
so natural in appearance that with a little imagination one
might fancy they could see smoke issuing therefrom.

Wild horses were occasionally seen in the distance. It was a
beautiful sight to see these wild denizens of the pathless Plains,
unfettered and unrestrained by bit or bridle, when, with flow-
ing manes and tails streaming in the wind, they would speed
away over the trackless prairie. Sometimes we encountered
small bands of Indians, who appeared peaceable and showed no
inclination to molest us in any manner. We exchanged courtesies with them, and often gave them food and refreshments, and
this, no doubt, served to lessen their hostility. And so we journeyed westward — ever westward — with thoughts of the Land
of Gold ever before us, and speculating as to what the outcome
of our adventures was to be.

Returning East—
My Marriage

Cold weather was now approaching, and our tents were none too warm for sleeping quarters. Our bedding and clothing, too, was becoming thin and threadbare. We all felt the fatigue of the long journey and were eager to see it end.

"The best of friends must part," and our parting soon came, having suffered no serious accidents or casualties, neither illness nor death having made any inroads on our party. We separated from the others after six months of travel which had been harmonious throughout. I never have met any of my fellow companions of that memorable journey since the day we separated.

After selling the cattle and stock, with the few horses we had used on the trip, we disposed of our camping outfit and kitchen utensils, and — most useful of all — our "Dutch oven." And here I must discourse for a moment on this most useful of camping utensils. How many good viands were cooked in our old Dutch oven! Hunters' potpies, biscuits, light and delicately browned, and that time-honored dish, baked beans. How delicious when prepared by soldiers or men of the West who "know how."

One of our drivers, who boasted that he could cook anything "From skunk to rattlesnakes, provided he had the stuff," wanted to try his hand at pie-making. He was as good as his word, so far as the pie was concerned. Gathering some buffalo-berries that grew in profusion over the Plains, and some ripe plums that were often found in the thickets, and with bacon fat in lieu of lard for shortening, he concocted a really appetizing pie, and it was eaten with real enjoyment.

One day this man wanted to try cooking a real "varmint," and proposed a rattlesnake to another of the drivers. Jim started out to locate a snake. These were so numerous that he had no trouble finding one. However, he was badly bitten while trying to kill the reptile, and in a short interval his arm was much swollen. My father applied restoratives and other remedies and in a short time the man recovered.

Our first objective point, after disposing of our effects, was San Jose — sometimes known in those days as the San Lorenzo Valley, near to and environed by the Sierra Madre Mountains. My mother's health was not improved by the climate, and my father, after waiting and hoping for beneficial effects, decided to remove to Sacramento, where he resumed his profession of medicine and engaged in mining enterprises. He also contributed various literary articles to newspapers and magazines, among the latter being Blackwood's Magazine, to which he had been a contributor for many years, not only because he was sought by this then-famous publishing house from ties of consanguinity, but for his literary ability, and because the senior members of the company at that time told him he had an inherited genius for writing.[3]

Two years after our arrival at Sacramento occurred the death of our mother. The home was therefore broken up, and

[3] *Blackwood's Magazine* was founded in 1817 by William Blackwood in Edinburgh, Scotland, and is published and edited to this day by a Blackwood descendant. No articles have ever been attributed to the authorship of one Dr. Thomas Blackwood.

my sister and I were consigned to the kind care of a clergyman and his wife who were returning to "the States." We embarked from San Francisco on the steamship "Golden Age," bound for New York. We were carried on the backs of natives across the Isthmus of Darien. At the end of another ocean voyage we landed in New York City, where we bade goodbye to our kind friends, resuming our journey by railroad back to our old home state of Michigan.

One year after our return came the news of the death of our father in California. We were therefore placed in the care of relatives — an uncle and aunt who were childless, and with them grew to adult years.[4]

I was educated in Albion, Michigan, at that time one of the most prominent collegiate institutions for young ladies. In the quaint, old-fashioned terms of the day it was famously known as a "Young Ladies' Seminary." A near-by town was Monroe, famous as the home of General George A. Custer, and it was while I was attending this school that I first met my husband-to-be. He was then on leave of absence en route to visit his home, and stopped off to see his sisters, Gertrude and Rowena, at the college.[5] He was then a captain in an infantry regiment. I was wonderfully impressed with the gallant warrior in his uniform and glittering braid, his fine appearance further enhanced by his military cape and the jingling spurs on his boots. He confessed to me afterward that he had put them on to impress the young ladies. Needless to say, he succeeded!

Our acquaintance, thus begun, ripened into warm friendship. My gallant knight, at the close of his leave of absence, hastened back to the front — for the Civil War was not yet ended — and I did not see him again until we became engaged

[4] Robert and Rebecca Blackwood lived in Northville, Michigan.

[5] Frank Dwight Baldwin, in May 1863, was a captain of the Nineteenth Michigan Volunteer Infantry on recuperative leave following his recent parole from a Confederate prisoner of war camp. After induction into the Nineteenth Michigan in August 1862, Baldwin served in Kentucky and Tennessee before being captured on March 25, 1863. For the next month Libby Prison at Richmond was his home until a prisoner exchange was arranged on May 6.

later. The wedding preparations were carried into effect to the satisfaction and admiration of the guests, and in the good old-fashioned manner of walking together down the stairway, preceded by the bridesmaids and my husband's best man. We took our places before the clergyman, who had known me from early years. This most important event in our lives took place on January 10, 1867.

Among the wedding guests was the old coachman of the family, Jimmie Sheridan by name, who had been, in his time, a great lover of horses as well as a judge of them. He could break or train the most fractious animal. As we passed by him into the drawing room, Jimmie grew reminiscent. He had heard of my officer-husband's war record — brave in battle, invincible and stubborn, and recalling my early attempts in girlhood at riding bareback, he said in a low voice — but loud enough to be heard in the waiting silence, "There they go! Pull, Dick, pull, Devil; you need halter-breaking, Alice, you sure do!"

Our honeymoon was spent on the way to my husband's regiment, the Thirty-Seventh Infantry — afterward consolidated with the Third and Fifth Infantry regiments, and stationed at Fort Harker, Kansas. We traveled as far as Junction City, then the terminus of the railroad. That was a trip never to be forgotten. It was in the dead of winter and bitterly cold, even in a Pullman coach, which was not always to be had. At no time were the cars comfortably warm. Conductor and train crew wore overcoats and spent no needless time with unnecessary details.[6]

[6] It took the wedding couple thirteen days to reach Junction City. Following an 11:00 A.M. wedding and reception, Frank and Alice immediately entrained upon a week-long round of visits among friends and family that included stops in Detroit, Coldwater, and Constantine. By the time Chicago was reached on January 17, all plans to go directly through to Kansas were scrapped because of the intense chill and fever suffered by the bridegroom. Refuge was taken at the home of Alice's cousin and the trip was not resumed until the twenty-first, and two days after that the end of the line of the Kansas Pacific Railway was reached. Frank D. Baldwin Diary (1867), Henry E. Huntington Library, San Marino, California. (Hereafter referred to as Baldwin Diary with the date.)

Fifty years ago Junction City was a typical western town. Cowboys, the like of which I had never seen before, rode yelling and whooping through the streets, displaying their dexterity by lassoing any creature that came along. They rode and plunged on their bucking chargers in front of the car windows, through which I gazed at them in wonder and amazement. It was on a Sunday when we arrived there, but there was no evidence in sight that it was the Sabbath Day. No church bells were to be heard; no gathering worshippers were to be seen, but crowds filled the saloons; dance halls were popular; gamblers, half-breeds and a motley multitude in general were plenty, and they were alarming to me, as well as to the tenderfeet and venturesome tourists who were in large numbers on the train.

None of us had been attracted or interested in the dreary, wind-swept Plains or the inhospitable appearance of the country. Sparsely settled and remote were those sod and log huts, too widely separated for neighborly activities or assistance if ever needed. Courage and fortitude must have been the strong incentive for these self-sacrificing and hardy pioneers of the remote West. Women forgot their timidity in the ever-to-be-feared Indian attacks and outbreaks, for more than once these natives had murdered and massacred, captured and destroyed, leaving nothing but cruel and hideous ruins and destruction behind.

After leaving the railroad, with its comparative comforts and necessaries, we climbed into an ambulance and drove out to Fort Riley, where we were welcomed by Colonel Reuben W. Barnard and his wife, a most hospitable pair, who were assiduous in their kind attentions. Their quarters were built of stone, as were most of the others. Comfortable in this haven of rest and safety, we remained for two days — a snow storm had arisen, and it was not considered expedient to travel until it subsided. I was not averse to remaining, under the circumstances, but my husband's leave of absence was nearly passed, and we had to go. He had made all arrangements to transport our personal possessions and baggage by "bull train" to our destination, Fort Harker, about 75 miles to the southwestward, or to be exact, on the Smoky Hill River, south of Ellsworth, Kansas.

A Prairie Roadhouse—
On to Fort Harker

We bade goodbye to our kind host and hostess, and drove out to a ranch kept by a man named Michael Hogan and his wife.[7] Here they conducted a sort of roadhouse, and did a good business. Drivers of bull trains, freighters, pony express riders and others who occasionally found their way to "Hogan's," weary and lost, were sheltered and given rest in this hospitable abode.

Hogan and his wife had a keen eye to business. The house consisted of three rooms — a large one the length and breadth of the house, with an immense fireplace, deep and yawning at one end of the "dining room," as it was called, and a kitchen, whose interior I did not see. There was one room overhead, extending the same length as the lower room, and reached by a ladder standing in the corner. But where were the bedrooms? No privacy at all; not even curtains to shut out the presence of

[7] The Hogan hotel at Salina was reached on Sunday evening, January 27, 1867. Baldwin Diary (1867).

the inmates who might be there. I observed two army cots on the lower floor, furnished with gray army blankets, but no sheets. Flour sacks stuffed with corn husks served as pillows.

The hour grew late, and I was both tired and sleepy. The group of men around the fireplace, enjoying its warmth and talking and singing, gave no sign of sleepiness or of climbing the ladder leading aloft. My husband remarked that possibly they did not want to "climb the golden stairs." I answered that it probably was the nearest approach to the golden stairs they ever would climb.

So we sat and sat and waited, but they took no hint of conditions. Then I ventured into the kitchen and asked the tired Mrs. Hogan if she would explain the situation to her lodgers and request them to step outdoors until the lady could undress and go to bed. This she did, and I was to give the "high sign" when they could all return to the warmth of the fire. The men all filed out into the snow storm, and when I had snuggled down between the blankets my husband told them they could come back and resume their cards and conversation.

Still there was no move toward the upper chamber by any of the others, and finally Hogan himself dispersed the inconsiderate guests by asking them if they "didn't know there was a lady present who wanted to sleep, even if they didn't."

The house cat with her brood of kittens had been making use of my blankets, and was cozily curled up in them, being somewhat rudely disturbed when I turned her out. Soon the cavalcade ascended the ladder and presently silence reigned, with the exception of the howling of wolves and the snoring of those on the upper floor. The dying fire made flickering shadows on the wall and over the humble surroundings. Unable to go to sleep, I indulged in fancy, and converted the log and mud shack into a stately feudal castle, with armed and girdled knights to defend and hold it against all intruders.

Sleep at length overpowered me, and with the dawn my romantic notions and imaginations vanished, when I saw the men descend from the room above. They did not seem to notice

that I was yet in bed, but one of them told me not to worry —
that they would turn their backs while I made my toilet, or they
would step outside, just as I preferred. Needless to say I chose
for them to step outside.

My husband was amused but politic with the Hogan board-
ers, for it was tactful and diplomatic to be more or less oblivious
to any inconvenience and lack of civilities and courtesies which
usually prevail in more polished circles; especially did it behoove
us to be so in our present situation, and in view of our long and
cold journey stretching out ahead of us to Fort Harker.

After a breakfast of bacon, biscuits and coffee with "long
sweetening," we made ready to start. I dreaded to leave my
warm shelter for the bitter cold, but there was no alternative.
So, wrapped in robes and blankets, with plenty of hay on the
floor of the ambulance to protect our feet as much as possible,
I was helped into the covered wagon, my husband admonish-
ing me to be brave and to remember that now I was a soldier's
wife. He sought by comforting words to reassure my waning
courage, as he took his seat beside me. The canvas at the rear
end of the ambulance was drawn tightly closed, but the cover
in front was open wide enough to enable the driver to see where
he was going. The open circle of canvas was about the size of a
porthole on a steamer, but it was sufficient to see the dreary,
snow-covered wastes all about us. In vain I sought to discover
some sign of hut or habitation. My "Young Lochinvar out of
the West" was smoking and discreetly silent, until at length he
remarked, "There, my dear, behold the site of your future
home; we will soon be there."

Eager and happy to be at last at the end of a long day's
journey, I looked but could see nothing through the thick snow
which had been falling all day. I could see no buildings nor any
sign of a "fort" until it was pointed out to me, but still could see
nothing but a spot elevated slightly above the rest of the landscape. A nearer approach disclosed a short stub of stovepipe,
although no smoke issued from its top. Presently I saw other
discolorations on the landscape, which proved to be the barracks

and officers' quarters. The so-called "barracks" were mostly dug-outs, but God be praised! there floating in the storm was Old Glory.

When at last we drove up to my "future home" I found it to be merely another dug-out. I exclaimed, "Why, where is our house?" and before my husband could reply, the sole occupant of the dug-out, who proved to be our "striker," came bustling up the few steps. He apologized and explained that he hadn't started a fire because the Indians had attacked the wood-train the day before, killing two soldiers, and they were "shy" of wood, but that had he known we were coming he would have managed to gather some odds and ends of wood to keep us warm. The honest fellow was profuse in his apologies, and really was concerned for my comfort and health.

Nobody in the garrison knew of our coming, so we found no preparations for our arrival. Fort Harker was far removed from all railroad or telegraphic facilities — not even a pony express rider had stopped to give the inmates of the forlorn garrison any news from the outside world.

KANSAS STATE HISTORICAL SOCIETY, TOPEKA

Fort Harker, Kansas, in 1867. The fort was established to distribute supplies to posts farther west and for operations against hostile Indians.

When I first entered my new abode I gazed with disgusted disappointment around the bare, squalid room. Its conveniences were limited to one camp chair, two empty candle boxes and a huge box stove, red with rust and grime, its hearth gone and the space filled with a tobacco-stained hill of ashes, the peak of which was surmounted by "chewed-out quids" of unknown vintage — but they were there! The sordid interior filled me with gloom, scarcely lessened by the four-pane glass window, dirty, dim and curtainless.

Exploring the "inner regions" I found the kitchen scarcely big enough to contain a stove, and such an array of cooking utensils as I had never before beheld lay on the dirt floor and on a packing box, which served duty as a kitchen table! The walls of the kitchen were stayed and supported by logs, while the ceiling was of the same material and covered with dirt. The logs had not been trimmed or cut off, and obliged one to bend low when passing underneath.

The "drawing room," as my soldier-husband facetiously called it, had a board floor, unplaned and full of slivers. Canvas covered the ceiling and dirt sides. It sagged slightly in the center and trembled under the scampering feet of pack-rats and prairie mice. The canvas cover not quite extending on one end, the pack-rats would perch on the beams, rear up on their hind legs, with their bushy tails hanging below, and survey me with their beady eyes. I was an unwonted (and probably unwanted) sight to them, and I am sure they were to me. But finally we became used to each other, although they raced and ran over my head, indifferent to my attempts to oust them with my broom.

My house contained the two rooms — the aforesaid kitchen and "drawing room," one end partitioned off by a portiere of gray army blankets. Behind this barrier was the sole bedroom accommodations of the dug-out. It was not exactly a "ladies' boudoir." Behind this retreat I cut a small hole in the gray blanket, through which I could peep at anyone who called whenever I sought privacy or had retired for the night.

A Bride's Trials—
Fort Harker Hospitality

That winter of 1867 was exceptionally bitter. The wolves, driven by hunger, were more numerous than usual, and often ventured within the garrison.[8] They howled, fought and yelped, even gnawing and scratching around the kitchen door. Stray scraps and refuse thrown out were devoured as soon as darkness fell and the beasts ventured forth. I was filled with terror at their ominous howling and proximity, and must confess to shedding many a homesick tear. Was it any wonder?

It was growing late in the afternoon when we reached the fort. The news of our arrival soon spread throughout the lonely

---

[8] The wolves very nearly killed Frank on his last day on duty in December 1866 before he went on furlough to return to Michigan and marriage to Alice. Caught alone on the prairie at night, Baldwin was surrounded by a large wolf pack and was saved from a terrible death only by skilled horsemanship, deadly accuracy with fifty rounds of ammunition, the deliberate sacrifice of his horse, and a chilling swim across the Smoky Hill River. See an unidentified newspaper clipping from 1900 entitled "Thrilling Encounter" in the Frank D. Baldwin Collection, Box 6, Henry E. Huntington Library. (Hereafter referred to as Baldwin Collection with box number.)

camp, and hospitable invitations were given us to make ourselves comfortable and take dinner at the officers' mess, which
we were glad to accept. Lieutenant Micah R. Brown of the U.S.
Engineers, accompanied us over to the log house, where I was
introduced to the officers assembled for dinner, prepared by
Mrs. Kelly, wife of the commissary sergeant. She was a kindly
soul, and her womanly heart at once divined the loneliness and
depressed feelings of the forlorn and homesick bride, and she
sought, by comforting and reassuring words, to console and
cheer; but her sympathies overwhelmed my fast-vanishing
spirits and fortitude, and to the embarrassment of all and the
confusion of my husband, I burst into tears, and wept into my
cove-oyster soup and deluged the baking-powder biscuits. I
could not recover my emotion, so my soldier, pitying me, and yet
half-provoked at my sobs, supported me back to my dug-out.

Twilight had come and the hour of "Retreat," and never
will I forget the scene, with the four musicians with fife and
drum, or the effect that the strains of "Fra Diavolo," played by
Bruno, the fifer, had upon me, as its melancholy sweetness
floated out, dying away over the dreary, snow-covered Plains.
I almost imagined "his fierce and swarthy form I beheld."

The following morning I concluded to have breakfast in our
own quarters — especially after remembering my outburst of
tears at dinner the previous evening. Joe Bowers, the striker,
had managed, by hook and crook, to "swipe," as he called it,
enough odds and ends of wood to start the kitchen fire. The top
of a box served as a table and a newspaper for a tablecloth, and
at the two plates were napkins made from the squares of flour
sacks, with the blue brands still on them; but they were clean,
fortunately, and so all discrepancies were excused.

The morning's repast could hardly be considered a feast, as
cooked by John Lick, a Dutchman, who served us with fried
bacon and apples, also stewed peaches and a concoction flavored with onions, with which I was unfamiliar. We also had
butterless toast of soldiers' bread, and coffee. The coffee pot he
placed upon the floor at my side. It was an immense affair,

holding a gallon or more, and evidently contained the "grindings" of previous and unknown dates, until it had reached the zenith of its capacity and completely filled the spout.

My Dutch "chef" offered to pour the coffee, but I refused his aid, being anxious to exercise my housewife's prerogative at this, our first meal in our own establishment; but alas, for my praiseworthy desires and attempts! When I tried to lift the coffee pot, my efforts met with disaster, for the clogged spout, suddenly released of its weight, spurted forth a hot and turbid stream that splashed over the front of my lovely gown, worn for this initial occasion. But my soldier admired and ate and petted and praised — presumably reminded of the episode and tears of the evening before; but when he went into the kitchen, where the two men had retreated, I judged by the emphatic language of the Lord of the Manor that all was not serene. But the interview had its good effects, for Joe cleaned house that day. The rusty stove was blacked, the floor swept and order generally restored.

During the day Post Surgeon Chase and his wife called. Mrs. C[hase] was confined to her bed the day of our arrival, and unable to meet me and bid me welcome. She was a very pretty and agreeable woman, and a warm friendship formed with that spontaneity which is often the characteristic of women's intimacies, not always lasting, I regret to state. But in our case, affection and love remained until severed by death.

Two miles away from the lower cantonment where we lived in temporary quarters, were two companies of infantry and one troop of cavalry. They were occupying fairly comfortable huts or houses on what was the site of the permanent quarters of Fort Harker, then in process of erection.[9] They were to be built of stone, and considering the period of time and the hundreds of

[9] Fort Harker was located on the left bank of the Smoky Hill River in August 1864, but removed one mile to the northeast in January 1867 to the present site of Kanapolis, Kansas. Robert W. Frazer, *Forts of the West: Military Forts and Presidios, and Posts Commonly Called Forts, West of the Mississippi River to 1898* (Norman: University of Oklahoma Press, 1965), p. 53.

miles which intervened between the fort and the railroad, the
quarters were really attractive and far more convenient and
commodious than the usual army quarters.

The commanding officer of the post was Colonel Dainger-
field Parker. Both he and his wife were delightful southern
people, and the souls of hospitality. They occupied a slab house
until their own quarters could be finished. The exterior could
in no way be distinguished from any of the others, but the
interior seemed like a sumptuous palace to me, with its curtains
and draperies of turkey red calico, bought at the post sutler's
store. There were buffalo robes to cover the rough flooring and
portable book shelves on the walls. Two low trestles on which
were placed boards, with a straw tick or mattress, was made
to do duty as a couch, and was both comfortable and beautiful,
with its bright Indian blanket.

The troop commander of the Seventh Cavalry was Captain
[Major Alfred] Gibbs and the post quartermaster was Lieutenant Wells Willard. This last officer and his wife occupied
a log house consisting of one room, which was drawing room,
kitchen, and bedroom combined. There was but one small
window, but it was plenty large enough to lighten the limited
space within and if small, and lacking in the plainest and most
necessary furniture and conveniences, the warmth of welcome
extended to the stranger within its gates was unbounded and
made up for all deficiencies.

Vigilant watch and guard was maintained day and night
against Indian attacks and marauding bands of horse thieves,
who roamed all over that section of the West at that time.

The intense cold continued, and the wolves, driven by hunger, grew bolder and bolder. Their ferocity was somewhat
quelled on one occasion by a fight between a Scotch stag-hound
and a huge Lobo. It was fought to a finish, and the hound
was the victor.

A social spirit was revived and a ball and dinners given in
honor of the bride and groom. The ball was unique and original,
considering much that was necessary to beautify and adorn, but

there was not a shop or store within hundreds of miles (save the sutler's store) that was available; so the four ladies of the fort conferred together, and combining tastes, brains and ideas, succeeded in making a "bower of beauty" out of a half-completed stone building — the unfinished portion eked out with tent-flies and canvas; the floor was covered with the same, and army blankets were hung over the windows that were to be. To be sure, the whole place was draughty; the wind blew through chink and cranny, but the two large box stoves, piled full of wood by the soldiers, together with the activities of dancing, kept everyone warm enough to be comfortable. The wood detail had returned this time in safety and without any interference by the Indians.

Around the spaces on the walls were place-cards with such inscriptions as "On with the dance," "Let joy be unconfined," "There will be no more weeping and sorrow *here*," the last accented by red letters. There was no band at the fort, so the company musicians, augmented by several civilian employees, took their places on the platform erected for the occasion. Violins, guitars and a wheezy accordion furnished the music, while Bruno with his whistling fife shrilled high over this conglomeration of sounds. The "Virginia Reel" and "Money Musk" — how everyone enjoyed them, thrilled both in hearts and heels. Forgotten for the time was absence of home and the associations of dear friends of the past on like occasions. The ladies wore their best "bib and tucker" and borrowed of each other and exchanged what one possessed and the other did not — a kindly spirit and mutual interest with us all.

The supper was bountiful and the cove-oyster patties equalled in memory those delicacies of the past. Good Mrs. Kelly was there to work and superintend the feast, assisted by a few "strikers." This latter term applies to those useful and necessary soldiers usually detailed in officers' quarters, who are an important adjunct to the comfort of those households, and always easily obtained, as their pay is increased thereby, with a satisfactory "stipend," and three meals daily, in warm and comfortable surroundings.

Joe Bowers, our family "factotum," even if willing and ever ready, did not, in minor details, such as dishwashing, coincide with my views of order and cleanliness. After broiling a steak he would put the gridiron in the bottom of the woodbox and carefully cover it up, assuring me, when I discovered this trifling error and remonstrated with him, that it was better for gridirons to be kept always greasy when not in use.

There was always plenty in the commissary to supply the table, augmented frequently by game given by some wandering and venturous hunters; the pot was always kept boiling. Wood was not always as plentiful as necessary to keep warm our breezy quarters, and on such occasions we would wrap ourselves up and go to bed to keep warm. Those were trying days, and one had to muster up all the fortitude one possessed to make the best of everything.

The bride and groom were entertained — not lavishly, perhaps, but none the less entertained, and heartily. At one dinner party to which we were invited, the house consisted of one room, which served as bedroom, sitting room, and kitchen combined. There was just space for the stove and a small stand on which to serve the dinner. The furniture consisted of three chairs and an iron cot, the latter used by the bride to sit on, while the groom occupied one of the chairs, the host another and the hostess the remaining chair — when not busy serving her guests. I watched her in admiration as she deftly fried ham, baked the potatoes, stewed the tomatoes in their can in a kettle of hot water, then opened the can and seasoned them, pouring them into a soup toureen, and we had a feast "fit for the gods."

Indian Captives Rescued— Scourge of Cholera

The long, dreary winter at length came to an end. The snow-covered prairies lost their mantle of whiteness and flowers reared their heads instead. There were varying shades of the wild hyacinth, with its purple clusters, the yellow daisies, the foxglove and the bright blossoms of the thorny cactus, while the green plains made all a scene of floral beauty which was most pleasing to the eye, after the monotonous winter.

The Smoky Hill River broke its icy barriers, and the huge cakes melted and disappeared; the cottonwood trees bordering its banks put forth their young leaves, and Spring in all her beauty was welcomed.

Rumors were afloat that an inspector was coming to look over the post, and everything was made ready. Cavalry and infantry, man and beast, were drilled; uniforms examined, brushed up and their decorations polished. The commanding officer said he could not afford to be caught napping.

One morning, shortly after reveille, who should ride into camp, with a rattling of sword and much display, but Major General [Winfield S.] Hancock, with a detachment of cavalry, on his way to New Mexico. There was no formal inspection. The general realized the situation of the isolated post, and his keen and practiced eye made no disparaging criticism.

After a rest of a few hours and a lunch, which we all attended, the general and his men resumed their march.[10] They crossed the Smoky Hill River without a mishap, and were soon lost to view. This incident was a wonderful diversion in the lonely lives of the inhabitants of Fort Harker. The general had told the commanding officer that great changes were coming in the near future. Troops were to be ordered elsewhere. Orders were issued to the quartermaster to hasten the completion of quarters, and the hitherto dull and quiet post became a scene of bustling activity.

Soon the quarters were finished, and we emerged from our dug-outs and log huts into our respective homes. We soon were settled and felt as if living in palace[s] compared to our former abodes. But not for long did we enjoy our comforts.

One evening my husband and I were talking before our cheerful fire. He was officer of the day. It was shortly before midnight when we heard the rattle of wheels outside. Some vehicle stopped in front of our house, shortly followed by a sharp, vigorous knock on our door. It proved to be Lieutenant G. A. Hesselberger of the Third Infantry, on his way to the railroad, the nearest point then being Salina, Kansas, about 40 miles distant from Fort Harker.

---

[10] General Hancock left Fort Riley on March 27, 1867, moving westward in search of hostile Indians. The purpose of the expedition was to give evidence of the strength of the federal government to the Plains tribes and punish those who invited war. This force of 1,400 men arrived at Fort Harker on April 1 and stayed but two nights. The general was not en route to New Mexico, but was restricted to Kansas and the Indian Territory. See Henry M. Stanley, *My Early Travels and Adventures in America and Asia* (New York: Charles Scribner's Sons, 1895), 1:3–47; U.S., Congress, Senate, *Senate Executive Document 13*, 40th Cong., 1st Sess., 1867, pp. 84–109.

In the ambulance at the door were two white women whom the lieutenant had rescued from the Indians, and he was taking them to their eastern homes. They had been captured, and for months had been living in revolting captivity. Now, after a long, perilous journey, the lieutenant had reached Fort Harker with his hapless charges, and sought shelter for the night. Needless to say, he got it. Everything possible was done for the pitiful creatures. They were two young women, sisters, who had met this awful fate. The elder girl, about twenty years of age, was in an indescribable plight — starved, beaten and abused, her sufferings culminated in making her a raving maniac. The other sister had not lost her mentality, and could give us — especially myself — an indescribable history of their life in captivity.

That night was one I shall never forget. Nearly all night the wretched maniac shrieked and raved over the awful sufferings she had endured, living over her terrible experiences. At one time she would appeal to us to save her and besought God to take care of her. The hospital steward, with the post surgeon, came and remained all night, and at length after sedatives had been repeatedly given the poor exhausted girl, she slept for hours undisturbed.

After remaining for two days and conferring with the commanding officer and my husband, Lieutenant Hesselberger considered it best to proceed on his journey to the railroad. He was given a strong escort of soldiers and a plentiful supply of ammunition. Eventually the captives reached their home in safety. I never heard of them again.[11]

[11] Margaret and Josephine Box, aged fourteen and seventeen, were ransomed by Lieutenant Hesselberger from the Kiowas for $2,800 worth of supplies at Fort Dodge. In August of 1866 their family had been attacked by Kiowas in Montague County, Texas, the father being immediately killed but the mother and four daughters taken captive. The infant daughter was murdered and another girl and the mother were traded to the Kiowa-Apaches, later to be recovered. See Corporal Leander Herron in Robert M. Wright, *Dodge City, the Cowboy Capital and the Great Southwest in the Days of the Wild Indian, the Buffalo, the Cowboy, Dance Halls, Gambling Halls, and Bad Men* ([Wichita: The Wichita Eagle Press, 1913]), pp. 120–29.

It was midsummer when we were visited by a scourge of cholera, most violent and relentless. As I remember, few escaped its ravages. Persons were smitten without warning, and so virulent was the disease that the living were unable to bury the dead.[12] At that time there were four officers' wives at the post, including myself. The wife of the post surgeon was the first to die, followed by Mrs. Chase, who died in childbirth. Mrs. Bell, wife of the commissary officer, and myself were the remaining women. Mrs. Bell, having a young child, was sent to her distant home, and I was then the sole surviving officer's wife at the post.

The cook of the post surgeon was the next to pass away. The evening before — and after the death of the post surgeon's wife — she had been over to see me, feeling as well as usual. That night she died. The first intimation of her death was when I walked out on the verandah of my house next morning and glanced over at the next set of quarters. I saw a row of something under a canvas covering, and one of them was poor Bridget, the cook! There they all lay, waiting to be interred in the lonely little makeshift cemetery. All were well and in their usual health only the night before!

News of our hapless plight reached Fort Leavenworth, and Sisters of Mercy, with two priests, were sent to our relief and succor. With tenderest care and attention, regardless of creed or creedless, they took care of and nursed the sick and dying, day and night, until the scourge had lessened and passed.

Among the victims were a sergeant and wife who left four little children, alone and homeless. The good Sisters took them to Leavenworth and provided for them. One of the priests fell a

[12] The cholera outbreak was epidemic among the Kansas posts. The carriers were infected members of the Thirty-Eighth Infantry marching from Jefferson Barracks at St. Louis to New Mexico. Four companies of the battalion reached Fort Harker between June 22 and 25, 1867, and on June 28 the first cholera case appeared at the post. Before the disease ran its course twenty-one persons died at Fort Harker. See Leo E. Oliva, *Soldiers on the Santa Fe Trail* (Norman: University of Oklahoma Press, [1967]), pp. 199–200; U.S., Surgeon General's Office, "Report on Epidemic Cholera and Yellow Fever in the Army of the United States, during the year 1867," *Circular No. 1*, pp. 28–49.

victim to the disease — Reverend Father Martyn. Daily he had
called on me to inquire after my welfare, and he always had a
word of cheer and comfort. My husband was away at this time
acting as escort for General Hancock.[13] Father Martyn had
been in the habit of visiting the little town of Ellsworth to ad-
minister to the sick and afflicted there. One evening a soldier
passed the dead body of the priest, lying on the ground, while
his mule grazed near by, midway between the post and the
town. He had been stricken while on his way home!

Not long had we recovered from the cholera scourge when
we were threatened with another evil. This was smallpox.
Colonel Henry Merriam of the Thirty-Eighth Infantry (colored), on his march to New Mexico, passed with his command
in which smallpox had developed. Fortunately the disease was
checked without any fatalities.[14]

Our lives were not at all devoid of other excitement. One
day a soldier came staggering into the post on his mule, which
dropped dead under him. The man had been pursued by Indians for twelve miles, and by hard riding had made his escape.
The heat that day had been unusually intense. Exhausted and
unable to sleep, after hours of effort, I arose and went to the
open window. The tragedies and events of the summer had
made me extremely nervous and filled me with forebodings.
Both windows and doors were kept open day and night to allow
as much air as possible. I sat on the window sill, wondering
what was the cause of the bright light in the sky away in the
direction of a rancher's home.

While speculating, a voice close at hand exclaimed: "What
are you doing there, Mrs. Baldwin? Go back to bed." It was
my neighbor across the hall, Major William H. Bell, commissary

[13] Baldwin's company of the Thirty-Seventh Infantry was assigned
escort duty to take General Hancock and his guests to Denver. They left
Fort Harker on June 6 and returned July 12 after a round trip of 844 miles.
Baldwin Diary (1867).

[14] The Thirty-Eighth Infantry was responsible for the cholera outbreak,
not the smallpox.

officer, whose wife and baby had fled the plague-stricken post some weeks before. The major, also, had been kept awake and was sitting in the open front door. While we were discussing the bright light that had attracted my attention, a soldier came running up and told us that the rancher's house had been attacked by Indians and set afire. Everything had been pillaged or destroyed. The rancher and one other man had been killed, and the man who brought us the news had escaped only by hiding in the brush bordering the Smoky Hill River. By swimming and wading he had crossed the stream and made his way to Fort Harker and spread the alarm.

Pursuit was out of the question, as the savages had too great a start after completing their devilish work. One of the sons of the slain rancher was a surgeon in the United States Army, attaining distinction as one of the foremost surgeons in the service.

Leave for New Mexico—
Indian Council at
Fort Larned

The old-time army quarters of fifty and more years ago were built with a common hallway. On either side were accommodations for two sets of quarters — in other words, two families under one roof — not always to be desired, and often productive of strained relationship between the occupants, frequently amusing and ridiculous, especially when there were children, or when the head of the house was late in getting home, and forgot to shut the door; or when, as officer of the day, he would yawn loudly and sleepily, and trail his sword or saber noisily over the bare floor.

Children and chickens were a never-failing cause of disturbance; also dogs, the latter often burying bones in a neighbor's attempted garden. The hens, addicted to scratching forays, found the soft loam of the gardens a tempting place. Then, too, suspicions would arise as to where the eggs disappeared. No direct charges were ever made, but insinuations tended to disturb the serenity of the neighborhood.

My neighbor across the hall was Major Bell, commissary officer, a delightful gentleman, intelligent and agreeable. He was a musician of no mean ability and a fine violinist. Often he would come over to our side, and sitting down on the floor with his eyes closed and back against the wall, would tuck his violin under his chin and pour forth sweet strains from "The Bohemian Girl," "La Sonnambula" and the Jewel Song from "Faust," while I listened with tear-filled eyes, recalling those past, happy times when I had heard the same ravishing strains under happier circumstances and surroundings than at an isolated army garrison in the heart of a hostile Indian frontier.

As expected, General John R. Brooke arrived, and preparations were made without delay for our departure for New Mexico. What a scene of activity and excitement! The troops jubilant and eager for the march; everybody in high spirits and ready for a change, for the past eight months had been monotonous, unvaried save by pestilence and the necessary duties of garrison life. All wanted to go — to be on the move — for fresh fields with their unknown allotment of weal or woe.

The troops were mostly young men with varying terms of service. The zest and vigor of youth was theirs. Ambition and inexperience defied alarm and apprehension.

Finally came the day of departure. Army wagons loaded with regimental property, government ambulances and one or more private conveyances owned by individual officers — our own ordered some months previously among them — drew up in line before the dismantled quarters, and the ladies and their households, increased by new arrivals during the summer, cooks, servants and belongings in general, took their places inside and were ready for the start.[15] Reveille sounded, and we were off on September 3, 1867, with General John R. Brooke in command.

[15] Each officer was allowed one wagon in which to transport his effects. The Baldwins were more fortunate than other families because in addition to the six-mule wagon they also had a privately owned Black Maria Coach, a gift of Alice's Uncle Robert Blackwood. In addition Alice took along her maid, hired in Leavenworth in May at the rate of $20.00 per month. Frank D. Baldwin, "Autobiography" (Henry E. Huntington Library), p. 269, and Baldwin Diary (1867).

It was early, the morning was cool, and the soldiers marched briskly to the beat of drum and shrilling of fife. After a march of eighteen miles we reached Plum Creek, tired and weary. The day had grown exceedingly hot and several of the men had suffered with sunstroke. No wood — not a stick of timber, did we see on the way, or a drop of water, save what we had brought along to drink, until we reached Plum Creek. The name, by the way, was a misnomer, for there were no trees in sight, save a few cottonwoods which made a scattered and meager shade from the glaring sun.

Here tents were pitched, beds made down, and we were soon stretched exhausted. Horses and mules were unhitched and were soon rolling and tumbling on the prairie and drinking their fill from the creek. Fires were lighted, coffee pots were soon bubbling, and the smell of frying bacon filled the air with appetizing odors, while soldier cooks were busy at the tailboards of their wagons making baking-powder biscuits.

I shall always remember that one initial meal eaten in camp on Plum Creek — the first of many such which were to follow for many weeks.

The next day was a repetition of the first, making an early start so as to cover as much ground as possible before the heat of the day came upon us. There was considerable delay in starting. One of the mules had wandered off, and when found was dead, and his body swollen to enormous size. The poor beast had been bitten by a rattlesnake. However, we finally got under way. We met nothing on this day's march but an ox train loaded with lumber. The Plains were nothing but a vast waste, hardly a weed even was to be seen, while the dust which arose from the moving column was stifling.

After marching fourteen miles we went into camp on Cow Creek, reaching there late at night. There was no wood with which to cook supper, so buffalo chips were used as fuel, a useful substitute when no other fuel was available. Nothing out of the ordinary occurred. Reveille sounded early, as was to be the case for many a day on that long journey, but on this day, word

came that the command would lay over for the day. Each of us
therefore busied ourselves in various ways, I with needle work
and letter writing to be mailed at the first available opportunity.
The troops busied themselves in various duties — mending their
clothes, reading and sleeping.

My soldier was officer of the day. The following morning
we made a comfortable march as the air was cool and bracing.
After fifteen miles we camped at old Fort Zara [Zarah], Kansas,
a forlorn and desolate place of two or three little mud and stone
houses, but now all in ruins, mute reminder of what had once
been a lively army post, but at this date a silent, uninhabited
spot.[16]

To add to the gloomy scene it began to rain, but fortunately
did not continue very long. Our faithful utility man, Bowers,
who served us all through the long march, found some strag-
gling wild plum trees, and to my own satisfaction as well as that
of others, we made pies and "sass," as Bowers called it, which
was a variety to the monotonous daily menu of baking power
biscuits and canned foods, generally and occasionally, as circumstances permitted, varied by fish and fowl, prairie chickens
and plover, or sometimes rabbits. These prairie tidbits, eaten
with the tart and juicy plum, were much enjoyed.

The nights were now getting chilly, making the evening
campfire, after a long day's march, a sociable and comfortable
gathering place. Someone in the circle would play on the banjo
or guitar and sing, and the rest of us would join in on the chorus.
In the moonlit and starlit nights, there was a quiet and serenity
in the atmosphere, despite the watchfulness for Indians or other
foes.

One day between Fort Harker and Fort Larned, we saw in
the distance moving objects. It turned out to be an ambulance
and escort of soldiers. The ambulance contained the body of
Lieutenant Henry Romeyn's wife, and the escort were accom-

[16] Fort Zarah, three miles east of the present town of Great Bend,
Kansas, though small, still had some inhabitants on September 6, 1867, as it
would not be abandoned until December of 1869.

panying the remains to the nearest railroad point, whence they were to be shipped to their old home in Michigan. It was a melancholy cortege, and all were more or less affected by the spectacle.

Approaching Fort Larned, we camped about a half mile from the post.[17] We all then went down to an Indian council which was being held at the quarters of Colonel [Edward] Wynkoop, agent, where we saw Tall Bull, Little Raven, Yellow Bear and Black Kettle. These Indians were Cheyennes and Kiowas. All sat in a circle, silently smoking, with the interpreter, a half-breed woman, Celestia Adams. She was a good-looking woman, with her white blood predominating in her features and general appearance. Colonel Wynkoop, with several officers, was seated in the circle. One of the women from among the traveling caravans seated herself next to Celestia, in spite of the latter's whispered remonstrances, and when the pipe of peace was passed around to each individual in the circle, she took a whiff herself, to the surprised consternation of her husband and the indignant chiefs. But it was done, and after asking Celestia to tell them to "come again," she withdrew from the circle. Black Kettle was insulted, and frowned with a malignant eye at the fun-loving white squaw. Possibly the presence of several hundred soldiers close at hand insured safety and protection. But it was an impolite imposition, nevertheless.

[17] On September 8, 1867, Fort Larned was the scene of preliminary talks between the Indian Peace Commission and hostile Plains tribes. In a few days the council would be moved, at Indian insistence, to Medicine Lodge Creek where a treaty would be signed in late October. Donald Berthrong, *The Southern Cheyennes* (Norman: University of Oklahoma Press, [1963]), pp. 289–97.

"Bootlegging" Under Difficulties— A Snake Incident

After the council was over, presents were distributed to the Indians, and bidding our host and his wife goodby, we returned to our camp, where we were later called upon by the few officers and their wives of the fort.

While we were talking and visiting with them, a most amusing incident occurred. Suddenly, to my astonishment and surprise, who should appear before us but Bowers, our striker, with a bottle of wine, some tin cups and a plate of biscuits, the latter sweetened and made tempting by a liberal sprinkling of dried currants within. With a low bow he handed to the ranking officer one of the cups, which was smilingly accepted.

After our callers had departed, I questioned the apprehensive "wine bibber" as to where he had procured the material for the liquor, and how he had made it. He said he had gotten the plums from the thickets quite a time before, and had carefully hidden them away, a few at a time. Then, after we had all gone to bed he had cooked them in the camp kettle until they were soft, then had added sugar, and straining the mess through a *sock* until it was clear, he had bottled it up for future use. He had succeeded in his efforts undisturbed, and owing to the caution and quiet of the camp and a bribe to the sentinel by a drink and a piece of pie, had succeeded in his "Volstead-able" act undetected.

At the time these plums were gathered, I had thought the supply did not last very long, but had asked no questions. However, I accepted the honest fellow's intentions, as they were meant to please me! But I admonished him, when serving a mixed company of guests, to wait on the ladies first — to which he listened with a doubtful air. His training as a soldier and his own ideas as to "woman's status" had not kept pace nor advanced to the high standard accorded them in this land. Incidentally, I kept secret the process of his wine experience — especially his method of *straining it*! Certainly it was original.

A strange incident took place on our next day's march. As the long line of troops were passing over the hot, dusty trail, the cavalcade suddenly stopped, while the ambulances and vehicles following behind came to a sudden halt. It appeared that an immense rattlesnake had coiled itself in the immediate track of the marchers. Various sorts of missiles were hurled at the intruder, to which no attention was paid. One of the men in the foremost ranks stepped forward until close to the reptile, then without a word or gesture, gazed fixedly into the eye of the snake. Suddenly it uncoiled and stretched at full length in the road, when the trooper, with a movement as quick as lightning, caught it behind the neck and hurled it into the air with two revolutions, breaking its neck. All this happened without a word or exclamation from the soldier, while the onlookers stared in astonishment at the recklessness of the man.

This incident created a profound impression upon all the troops who had witnessed it. The soldier was a quiet, unobtrusive sort of a chap, faithful in the performance of his duties, and no complaint had ever been registered against him in any manner. He was a young man, of peculiar and extraordinary physical appearance, well built and athletic. But it was his head and face that repelled one. His hair was coal black — no trace of African blood — in fact, the negro servants in the command declared he was "no nigger." But his eyes were what baffled and confused all who looked at him. They were pale and gray, with a shifting light in their glance, and were overshadowed by brows thickly grown until they met over his nose. All this was set in a swarthy face, neither mulatto nor quadroon. An officer in the command confessed that the man's eyes baffled him, and gave him a nameless fear when looking into them. This man was never "hail-fellow-well-met" with his comrades, and although they never made other than a curious criticism of him, they avoided him, and ostracism was complete and entire. One morning at roll call the man was missing. He had deserted. No effort was ever made to locate him, nor was he ever heard from again.

Various opinions and speculations were indulged in by the command after the snake incident, as to the power he possessed over the reptile. Bowers was of the opinion that he had the "evil eye."

The "charming" of the snake had a depressing effect upon all, particularly the ladies; but we were to be further alarmed and unspeakably horrified. Not more than a mile from where we had gone into camp was the scene of a fight between Indians and a wagontrain of ammunition stores and goods, which had taken place three days previously. The bodies of men, savagely mutilated, were lying around, with dead oxen and an empty wagon. Our chaplain volunteered the cheerful information that "We are liable to be attacked at any time."

We stopped long enough to give the bodies Christian burial, and brief services of prayer were conducted by the chaplain at the graves.[18] He had joined us at Fort Larned with his family. He was Chaplain J. A. M. La Tourette [Tourrette].

It rained continuously during the night, while the wind blew a gale, threatening to blow the tents down. Next day the storm

---

[18] Four bodies were buried. Baldwin Diary (1867), entry by Alice Baldwin.

abated, but the ground was soft and wet. We could not kindle
a fire, so we went to bed again to keep warm and dry. During
this enforced rest we heard a discouraged soldier singing, "I
want to be an angel and with the angels stand." His melody
died down in the distance, as he led his mule to water in the
turbid Arkansas River, which we had followed. His song was
followed by an exclamation from a fellow soldier that "He stood
a better chance to warm up in Hades than he did with the
spooks in the other region."

The soldiers would joke in the face of death itself. Reckless
and blasphemous in speech, defying any earthly power, they
were ready for whatever came along.

We marched eighteen miles during the day to reach Fort
Dodge, a comfortless-looking place, where we were joined by
several officers and their families. This military post, built some
years after Fort Harker, was not as commodius or well supplied
with quarters or equipment as was that post.

We did not linger longer than was necessary to refresh both
humans and beasts. Here we secured a few supplies such as
fresh milk and loaves of bakers' bread — sweet and delicious —
and a refreshing change from condensed milk and baking-
powder biscuit. The water at Dodge also was good and refreshing, after drinking the tepid and brackish water of the Arkansas.

While at Dodge, Lieutenant [Henry] Karples and wife and
Lieutenant William Gerlach called. Also the hospital steward
sent me a dozen eggs, which were most gratefully received and
relished. Had they been nuggets of gold they could not have
been more appreciated.

After passing Dodge we went through a prairie dog village
fully a mile long. Grashoppers also were a scourge, and at times
the air was filled with the pests.[19] Occasionally we rested from
our marches, and were glad of the chance, as all were in need
of it. I read "Frederick the Great and His Court," by Miss

[19] On the third and last day at Fort Dodge, September 14, Alice found
"the grasshoppers are numerous as ever, eating holes in our clothes and
today when I was asleep one bit me on the lip and made me mad." Ibid.

Muhlbach — more to pass the time than for any other reason, as I had read it before.

Indians were seen on this day's march, and a detail of men were kept out as guards. We marched twenty-one miles and camped on the banks of the river in a valley. At this place I saw a wild horse — a snorting, timid creature, which took to his heels after one frightened stare, pursued by the dogs in camp which returned with lolling tongues after a futile chase.

The days were all alike, monotonous and tedious, varied occasionally by the mules stampeding. One man sustained a broken leg one day, and several others were more or less injured by accidents of one kind or another. The stampede was caused by an officer on a white horse galloping along the line. During this bit of excitement, most of the dishes in the mess chest of Brevet Lieutenant Colonel V. K. Hart, Seventh Cavalry were broken, while not a single one of my newly-acquired eggs was even cracked! Bowers had traded a bottle of his "wine" with a laundress at Fort Dodge and secured three hens and a rooster in exchange. They were carried in a crate in the rear of the ambulance, where the rooster crowed in the early morning, and the hens fulfilled their mission in life by an occasional egg — which, by the way, the wily, pillaging colored cook of one of our camping neighbors would watch his chance to steal. Bowers caught him in the act one day, thrashed him "within an inch of his life," and took the precious hen fruit away from the culprit.

Often the weather was chilly, and drizzling rains and fogs prevailed; yet it was a relief from the hot arid winds which swept over the Plains. The prairies, too, were broken in their flat monotony by hills and grassy dales, wherein birds of various species sang and rested. Coyotes, too, were quite numerous, and hovered about as scavengers in the wake of humanity. The Lobo wolf was not often seen. Antelope occasionally showed themselves. They were graceful creatures, and one was killed. I would much better have enjoyed the juicy steaks if I had not previously seen the soft, beautiful eyes of the victim.

Another day, my soldier started out, after camp had been made, to seek what he could for the larder, and came back with two ducks, which were greatly enjoyed with the canned currant jelly. There was much enjoyment sitting around the lid of a mess chest which had been converted into a table, eating the meal prepared by the soldier cook, sometimes in top boots and spurs and with a gun in his belt.

On to
Fort Wingate,
New Mexico —
Birth of Little Juanita

And so the time wore on. The days were much the same and we were fortunate in keeping well. The surgeons and physicians had few duties in their line to perform.

The command finally arrived at Fort Lyon, Colorado, near Las Animas and all were glad to get there after our long and tedious march.[20] We camped some distance from the Purgatoire River, or, as it was pronounced in western parlance, "Picketwire."

The post was in command of Captain and Brevet Brigadier General W. H. Penrose of the Third Infantry. The quarters were of stone with high ceilings and bow windows — unusual and, to us, quite elegant. The site of the fort was a pleasant one and quite extensive. Captain and Mrs. [Edmund] Thompson called upon us and invited us to dine. The guests included

---

[20] When Alice arrived at Fort Lyon on September 25, 1867, the post was practically new, having been established on June 9 as a replacement for nearby Fort Wise.

several officers and their wives of our regiment. We were treated to wine and cake — the latter being an unusual luxury. Best of all, we actually had a fine tablecloth with napkins, which we certainly enjoyed, after eating off mess chests and bare boards so long.

When we started on the next day, my soldier and I drove ahead to Boggs' ranch. We almost tipped over in crossing the river. After passing through a grove of cottonwood trees we crossed a rustic bridge and came in sight of the ranch and an adobe and stone house, long and rambling in appearance. The owner of the ranch had lived there for twenty years, braving the dangers and insecurities of the Far West, and by endurance and continual labor had overcome almost insurmountable obstacles. He had prospered and was now comfortable and independent as far as the future was concerned. He was a bachelor. His household was managed and controlled by an old colored woman, his "mammy," for Boggs was a southerner, and the faithful old servant had followed her master through weal and woe. We were given generous quantities of fresh butter and cream, with milk, lard, vegetables and melons. Mr. Boggs refused payment for anything.

On the return, Burns, our driver, nearly tipped us over again, and failing in this, he fell out himself. He had been indulging in "the cup that cheers," not wisely, but too well.

The road we passed over was most picturesque, with vast quantities of rock massed in sublime confusion. Crossing the river we camped in a grove of trees. My soldier went fishing and brought back a fine rainbow trout, which was broiled and eaten with "caper sauce," concocted by the cook out of canned milk and pepper sauce.

At this point I washed a little puppy which had been given to me at Fort Lyon. It was covered with fleas, and I used tobacco-water with good effect. Here Paymaster [Major] Rodney Smith, who had arrived about midnight, paid off the men.

The next day's march was most fatiguing. The roads were rough, down precipitous gullies and up steep ascents. To add to the general discomfort, cactus was everywhere. The ground was sandy, which my soldier said was to be preferred to mud. General Brooke with Colonel Verling K. Hart called.

At length, after a weary and tedious journey of one month, over the alkali, wind-swept plains and prairies of that region, we marched, on October 4th, into the squalid little town of Trinidad, Colorado, whose adobe houses, interspersed with a collection of tents and wicky-ups, scattered over the adjacent hills and ravine.

After resting and recuperating for three days, the troops resumed the march of several more hundred miles, the objective point being Fort Wingate, New Mexico. We remained at Trinidad with a detachment of ten soldiers as guard and escort.

On the twelfth of October, 1867, under the shadows of Fisher's Peak, a baby was born to us. I was skillfully and tenderly cared for by a Mrs. [John D.] Kinnear, at that time the only American woman in the town. This baby was the first white child of unmixed blood born in Trinidad. She grew up to a beautiful womanhood, and in the vicissitudes and changes of army life, married, and herself became the mother of two children, born in Colorado, not remote from her own birthplace. Years after, she visited the aged Senora Felipe Baca, who was greatly interested in the young mother when her baby was born and who vied with the excellent Mrs. Kinnear in kindness and friendly ministrations. Senora Baca in her youth — and as she was then — was a beautiful woman with the black and lustrous eyes of her race. The interview between the young American and the descendant of proud hidalgos was inclined with sadness, for the once-while vivacious beauty had succumbed to the infirmities and mental incapacities of age. Mrs. Walker, daughter of "Uncle Dick" Wooten [Wootton], was present, and acted as interpreter for the two ladies as neither could converse with facility in the other's language. She it was whose hospitality and merciful ministrations years before gave succor and consolation when sorely needed.[21]

Time has wrought prodigious changes since those memorable days of 1867. Trinidad is now a city of importance whose private residences and public buildings can compare in architecture with its rival, Denver, or any other city in Colorado. The melancholy howl of the coyote, aforetime heard in the echoing darkness, and rattle of stage coach, with crack of whip and galloping mules as it clattered up with whoops and shouts and often a shot fired by a bibulous passenger, are sounds now banished by the chime of church bells, whistle of locomotives and rumble of Pullman coaches over the greatest railroads on the continent.

The baby born in Trinidad, Juanita, married in 1893, Ambrose C. G. Williams-Foote, an English gentleman of Honicomb House, Calstock, Cornwall, England. (See "County Families of England.") Soon after their marriage he became a citizen of the United States. In the Spanish War he was commissioned a First Lieutenant of Infantry (Eighth Immunes) and made Adjutant, Colonel Eli L. Huggins commanding. The lieutenant later was a First Lieutenant Thirty-Second U. S. Volunteers, Colonel L. A. Craig commanding. After arduous and distinguished service in the Philippines he was discharged and commissioned in the Philippine Scouts, from which organization he was some years later discharged for disability. He died May 31, 1922. This couple had four children: Baldwin, Gloucester (A. C. G. Junior), Alice Aimee, and Pierson Locke.

The main command of troops arrived at Fort Union, New Mexico, November 5, 1867. The detachment of soldiers left behind at Trinidad arrived later, with the little new recruit. Owing to my illness we had been obliged to remain for several weeks, but left eventually for Fort Union December 23, 1867,

21 Felipe Baca and his wife were sheep ranchers of considerable importance. Louise Kinnear was the common-law wife of John Kinnear, Trinidad's dance hall operator and sometime deputy marshal. The Baca home in which the Baldwin child was born is presently being restored by the State Historical Society of Colorado.

and made the entire distance in an ambulance, arriving at Fort Wingate late at night, January 31, 1868 [December 31, 1867].[22]

It was a weary trip over an uncertain and but little-known road, seldom traveled by private conveyances. Owing to the isolated and remote location of Fort Wingate, one of the oldest posts on the frontier, commissaries' and quartermaster's supplies were transported there by bull or mule trains. Occasionally solitary and isolated ranchers were seen who were, in every instance, glad to see us and were hospitable so far as their limited means and conditions permitted. Few women or children were among these dwellers of mud huts and dugouts. I was amazed to find an atmosphere of cheer and good humor among them, in spite of the adverse conditions under which they existed.

The weather had been mild enough to enable us to travel in comparative comfort. Our ambulance, made to order in Leavenworth, Kansas, was fitted up with comforts and conveniences. It had soft, upholstered seats that were extended when required and served as beds at night and as seats by day. The floor was covered with straw, over which rugs were laid to keep out as much of the cold as possible.

The baby, too, lay snug and safe when taking her nap in her little swinging hammock suspended from the ceiling of the ambulance by straps. The blankets and bedding were stored inside the seats during the day.

On the entire journey from Fort Union to Fort Wingate, lasting eight days, we traveled in our comfortable quarters.

[22] On the twenty-first of October Alice and the baby were well enough to travel and so continued the journey to Fort Union. One day's effort, however, weakened Alice and the family sought refuge in the home of the legendary fur trader Uncle Dick Wootton and his daughter near Raton Pass on the Colorado-New Mexico border. Frank left his wife here and went on the remaining fifty-six miles to Fort Union. He returned later when she was stronger and the journey was renewed on November 2. Fort Union was reached by the afternoon of the fifth. On December 23 the Baldwins left Fort Union to rejoin Frank's outfit which had meantime been transferred to Fort Wingate. They arrived at Fort Wingate December 31, 1867, rather than January 31, 1868, as Alice indicated. The Baldwin "Autobiography" (p. 278) states that Fort Wingate was reached the evening of January 5, 1868. See also Baldwin Diary (1867).

When we reached the ranch of some solitary homesteader we improved the occasion by buying our meals and stocking up on whatever was needed in the way of supplies, such as eggs and bacon. I observed that all these isolated dwellers had poultry.

We carried a spirit lamp and a coffee pot, and could thereby make coffee whenever we chose, and with a platter of bacon and fried eggs we were able to keep the hungry "wolf from the door."

At the little town of Cubero we halted long enough to partake of a meal of tamales and fried chicken. The "town" consisted of perhaps a dozen tumbling adobe huts, and the appearance of the entire place bespoke dire poverty. A Mexican woman, squatting on the outside of a house, eyed us silently, then arose and coming forward, accosted us in Spanish. Seeing the baby in her hammock, she broke into voluble speech. Taking our little daughter in her arms, she led the way into the house, and then and there prepared a meal for us, although we had to wait until the chicken was killed.

At this place we saw a number of Navajo Indians — for we were now in their country. My nurse and maid-of-all-work was much alarmed, and I also had my fears, but nothing happened to increase them. It was some time after dark — no moon to light our way and no stars, and it seemed to me that we had lost our way. We nearly tipped over once, but a huge hummock alongside the road prevented the ambulance from going over completely. We had to climb out while the driver and my soldier righted things and started us on the road again. During this process I took position on a box, while the nurse held the baby, the latter happily asleep.

We were far distant from Cubero, and did not know how far it was from Fort Wingate. Fortunately we discovered lights in the darkness, and apparently not far away. What a relief! Safety and succor were near at hand. The driver, unhitching one of the mules, mounted him, and following the direction of the lights, which were beacons of promise, he managed to reach the fort. Here he reported the plight of the wayfarers to the commanding officer, Colonel V. K. Hart, who at once sent out a team and soldier to guide us into the garrison. We were provided for with the rudest of conveniences as to room and beds — and an empty room in another house — a fireplace built in one corner with a bright fire burning, no bedroom furniture, not even a hospital cot for any of us.

Army blankets and sheepskins were in plentiful supply. They were spread on the dirt floor whereon we stretched our weary bodies and sought rest and repose as best we could. However, we got but little sleep, for the "pestilence that walketh by night" pursued us and made us sacrificial victims.

Numerous apologies were made by our host and his wife for the lack of accommodations, but as they had not been informed of our coming they could not be blamed. The post surgeon, Dr. R. S. Vickery, assured us — almost with tears in his eyes — that he would have sent over hospital cots had he known of our coming. But we survived all the omissions and difficulties.

Arrival at
Fort Wingate—
Monotony of Garrison Life

Fort Wingate at that time was one of the most remote military posts on the frontier. Two troops of the Third Cavalry and one company of the Thirty-Seventh Infantry, with the usual complement of officers, composed the garrison. The officers' quarters were built of adobe, one story high. The men's quarters were much the same. The fort was surrounded by a stockade of logs, with loopholes at intervals for firing through if besieged by Indians.

At one end of the square was the blockhouse, with a flat roof, on which a sentinel was posted night and day. Around this square was a moat, except at the sally-port or entrance, which was always guarded. It was evident that when this fort was first erected, the entire country was inhabited by hostile Indians. The Navajos were threatening and powerful, ready for attack and revenge against their encroaching enemies. Their war chief, Barboncito, had grown old and disabled, and his next in power was blind, and this once powerful nation had dwindled

Fort Wingate, New Mexico, in 1890. Established in August of 1860 and originally named Fort Fauntleroy then later Fort Lyon, the fort was withdrawn in September 1861 because of a Confederate invasion of New Mexico. Reoccupied in June 1868, the post was designated Fort Wingate.

down by disease and death to a few scattering bands of half-starved, wretched Indians and half-breeds.

Desertions from this post were frequent. I witnessed my first spectacle of this sort at Wingate. Two soldiers, an Englishman and an American, had deserted, but were captured, and were sentenced to have one side of their heads shaved and to be drummed out of camp to the tune of "The Rogue's March," "Poor old soldiers, poor old soldiers! Tarred and feathered and sent to hell, because they wouldn't soldier well!" The culprits were marched ahead of the drummer and fifer who followed closely behind them in line, the drummer beating and rattling his sticks furiously, while the fifer whistled away for dear life the ignominious and insulting air, as the entire garrison looked on. When the two deserters had reached the boundary line between the military confines and the surrounding country, the Englishman doffed his cap, turning the shaved side of his head toward the spectators and gave a mocking salute and a bow, shouting out that he "hoped we would all meet again." The other man said nothing but went his way, and we saw them no more.

While at Wingate the post was attacked by Indians, who tried to stampede the herd of cattle that gr_ _ed on the reservation. We were settling ourselves for the night. I was already in bed. Our soldier cook had gone to his bunk in a corner of the kitchen. My soldier was preparing to turn in when the "*long roll*" beat — dreaded sound! never heard except as a signal of danger. Shouts and noise sounded without, supplemented with orders and oaths and whoops and yells.

My soldier was ready in an instant, it seemed to me, and summoning the soldier cook, who appeared at once with, "All ready, sir," he called the two dogs and bade them stand watch in my room while he was absent. He warned me to extinguish the fire and keep as still as possible. Then they dashed out into the darkness.

I arose and dressed, but forgot to put out the fire. I was afraid to be in the dark alone, if the truth must be told. I listened to the pandemonium without and to the shouting of the captains. I was surprised at my own composure. I had read and heard that women had hysteria and swooned and were bathed in tears in times of danger. I felt that I was not at all romantic, because in the midst of my solitude I bethought me of eating a piece of pie — which I did! The baby was sweetly sleeping in her cradle, which the company carpenter had fashioned from a candle box, and the two dogs alternated between the cradle and the threshold of the door, whining and coming to me to lick my hands as if to apprise me that I was safe with them.

Finally the noise and uproar died away, the door was suddenly pushed open, and there stood my soldier. Glory be to God! Safe and sound, with the cook behind him. Nothing more serious had happened than an attempt to steal the post herd of cattle. Then I had a sort of relapse, and wept and sobbed and went into hysterics. Sympathetic Dr. Vickery came and quieted my nerves and restored me to my normal self, while the men folks praised and complimented me on my pluck. I was helped into bed, but spent a sleepless night.

Life at Wingate was monotonous. No social functions ever were held. The nearest settlement was Albuquerque, at that time a small but lively town. Cubero, a lonely spot, composed of but a few ramshackle adobes, was more or less in fear of Indian attacks, as the savages would descend upon them and steal whatever they could lay hands on in the way of food or provisions. The country for miles was devoid of any natural beauty, scarce and sparse as regards trees or foliage, and only goats and burros roamed in numbers over the barren land, although a few sheep were occasionally to be seen.

The Mexican inhabitants lived principally upon what they could derive from bartering and selling their animals. No cows were there to afford milk, but goat's milk in plenty was to be had. We found it health-giving to invalids, and especially to babies and children. The water was full of alkali, causing much thirst and discomfort for man and beast.

The Mexicans and their families living in proximity to the fort were friendly, as they knew they would be safe and protected by the soldiers if threatened by danger. The women were willing to serve in any way. Many of them were fine laundresses and of course were adept in preparing Mexican dishes. Mush and goat meat, with a seasoning judiciously flavored with green peppers, then fried, and encircled with hard-boiled eggs, made a dish both unique and appetizing. Even the ever-present cove oysters, eaten and endured because of their canned approach to the "real article," could be converted, by the addition of cracker crumbs and eggs, into a most delectable dish.

Game was scarce around Fort Wingate. Occasionally a wild turkey was brought in and sometimes a sage hen, but the latter was usually so strongly flavored with sage as to be unfit to eat. Ducks were plentiful and always to be found at a certain spring or pool about two miles from the post. This particular spot seemed to be their favored rendezvous.

An officer [Lieutenant Peter D. Vroom] who was a good shot and fond of hunting and fishing was thrown from his horse one day by the animal suddenly shying and pitching his rider into the spring. He came back to the post, wet and "duckless," and was laughed at by his good-humored brother officers — which I resented, because the officer had gone out after ducks to obtain enough of them to make a bed of down for the garrison baby, little Juanita Baldwin. This spring was ever afterward known as "Vroom's Folly."

Experience with a Cloudburst — Thanksgiving Time

After being stationed at Fort Wingate a year, orders came in 1868 to evacuate this post and establish a new one forty-odd miles west, on the site of old Fort Fauntleroy, which had been abandoned for many years. New quarters were to be erected as hastily as possible to enable the garrison and troops to move in. The new post was to be known as "New Fort Wingate." [23] Much was accomplished toward the erection of quarters in a brief time, and these were ready to move into as soon as we arrived. The sutler's store, a long, low, rambling building, lent an appearance of stability and importance to the surroundings.

This old-time sutler's store, with its roughly-hewn counters and dirt floor, with shelves containing a motley supply of goods

[23] Old Fort Wingate was established in 1862 in preparation for a campaign against the Navajo. Fort Fauntleroy was located some miles away two years earlier, but troops were withdrawn in 1861 because of the Confederate invasion of New Mexico. In June of 1868 this site was reoccupied by troops from Fort Wingate who affixed to it the name of the post they had just left.

of every description for the garrison in general as well as for the
needs and benefits of wandering civilians, was an interesting
spot. All sorts of goods were to be found there, from blankets,
bridles, lariats and calico for the squaws, to molasses, hardtack,
bacon and other eatables for those who chose to buy or sometimes "swap" for other goods.

And not to be forgotten was a "little back room," sacred to
the officers when in need of benign retirement. Also to prepare
themselves with explanations to their questioning and waiting
wives.

The Indians gathered at the sutler's store, which was always
an attractive place for them. There, silent and observing, they
would take note of everything, standing for hours with their
blankets around them, and covering one side of their heads and
faces, exchanging between themselves an occasional remark,
always guardedly, as there were interpreters who understood
what they were talking about and who could give warning of
any serious or threatening conversation.

The quarters for the officers had flat roofs and vent spouts
for the water to escape through, but even at that, when it rained
the roofs leaked like sieves, and the rainy season was now at
hand. Then there was confusion and discomfort in plenty. The
rooms consisted of three — including bedroom, partitioned off
from one end of the "dining and banquet hall," as my good-
humored husband called it, by the ever convenient army blankets. This "room" was just large enough for a bed, one chair
and a fireplace in one corner, with a small stand near to the
two-paned windows. The baby's cradle stood near the bed.

On one occasion the "heavens broke loose," and a deluge
was upon us. There was not a dry spot in the house. The rains
descended and the floods came in a turbid torrent. The ceiling
in my bedroom was converted into a waterfall. These leaks were
no ordinary affairs, but a shower to the right of us and to the left
of us. In bed, surrounded by basins, pails, tubs, cups, and
dripping pans — any available container to catch the water —
I lay motionless, not daring to move for fear of upsetting the

various receptacles. The room was too small to move the bed to a dryer place. The baby was snug and dry in her cradle, over which an umbrella was suspended. So passed the night!

The next morning the carpet in the front room, sodden and muddy, was a sight to behold! But all things must have an end, and the morning broke bright and clear. The sun shone brilliantly, and my husband and I, taking advantage of the fair weather and the genial warmth of the morning, started out for a walk and survey of our surroundings. We were down in a valley when we observed a black cloud looming suddenly over our heads. Without warning this developed into a cloudburst, and the previously peaceful scene was suddenly transformed into a sweeping, roaring flood. We ran for high ground. A near-by friendly Indian caught up with us, and my husband signaled for him to help him in forming a chair of their hands, into which I sat, and with my arms around their necks, I was carried to safety.

As we came near our quarters we observed the soldiers, with trousers rolled knee-high, bareheaded, carrying out armfuls of muddy hay that had covered the puncheon floor, while around outside stood the furniture, save the kitchen stove and the baby's cradle, the little one herself in the arms of my faithful but swearing striker. The house itself was deluged again, already having so many leaks that it could not possibly have been much worse. The only wonder was that the cloudburst had not demolished the adobe walls completely.

Among our effects was a parlor organ. It had afforded us more or less pleasure in our curtailed and limited accommodations. Here it was, leaned up against a tree with a piece of canvas over the top, and I looked at it with much apprehension, confident that it was now a wreck. I found, however, that the canvas had protected it nicely, and was thankful for small favors under such trying circumstances.

Willing hands, and plenty of them, soon restored order and a semi-comfortable condition. Bonfires were lighted, which with the aid of the sun, speedily dried out our blankets, carpet

and clothing. We had to make the best of our conditions —
there was no alternative.

We received our mail once a month, conveyed by the Pony
Express.[24] The road leading to the post wound through the
valley and around a point of rocks that hid from view the
approach of anyone, and not until well on its way could we see
the welcome sight of the mail carrier and his trusty, tired horse,
and then, with a whoop and a wave of hats and cheers from the
waiting crowd, he was received after delivering his precious mail
pouch to the commanding officer.

How eagerly we all read the stale news, for by the time the
isolated inhabitants of this well-nigh forgotten community
received it, all had become ancient history. With what anticipation every item was scanned. Newspapers were begged and
borrowed and read and passed down the line.

One day a Mexican came into the garrison, his burro loaded
down with vegetables, and stopped in front of the officers' quarters. To the eager ones who had for months subsisted on canned
food, dried apples, and no butter at all, this ragged, pock-
marked Mexican, with that load of vegetables, looked like an
angel of deliverance. In a trice almost he had sold out the bushel
of potatoes, for which he charged ten dollars, and the sack of
parsnips, together with a dozen hens and a dozen or more eggs.
He departed with more money in his pocket than he had ever
had before, and was quite elated and profuse in his promises to
come again.

Thanksgiving we endeavored to make as much like a home
dinner as possible, and also just as appetizing. To be sure we
missed the delicious dainties we had been used to in the East —
including the mince pies. But I was not to be entirely without
that national dish — fit companion to the roast turkey. "Necessity was ever the mother of invention," and I found my way out

[24] The legendary Pony Express which ran from St. Joseph, Missouri, to
Sacramento, California, operated for only eighteen months in 1860 and
1861. The reference here is to the Star Route riders contracted by the
federal government to deliver the mail to remote areas.

of my culinary difficulties with more success than I had anticipated. For my mince meat I had all the necessary ingredients except apples and brandy. Spices I had, by lucky foresight, supplied myself with from Santa Fe, when on our way to Fort Wingate. As a substitute for apples, I took the dried fruit (inhabited more or less by worms!) The damaged fruit was cleansed and made fit by numerous washings, and after soaking for forty-eight hours, spiced and given the addition of raisins — which had cost Uncle Sam eight dollars a box, and they were not seeded or seedless raisins, either! The soldier cook was pressed into service and overcame all omissions. But where was the brandy? Nothing but whisky to be had, and with the citron and other substitutes for improving the mince meat, we managed to get them in the oven.

Those pies were a triumph of art over nature. And the turkey! A nobler bird of his species never was seen. Barboncito,[25] our friendly Navajo Indian, had presented me with this one, a young bronzed gobbler weighing twenty-five pounds after being dressed; fat and tender and juicy in the skilled hands of the cook. This *piece de resistance* was flanked by a dish of mashed potatoes saved from those purchased from the Mexican some weeks previously. By hiding them under my bed covered with a blanket, I had managed to save them for this auspicious occasion. Then there was giblet gravy and onions in the turkey dressing, which, with pickles, currant jelly and cranberries, and the mince pie and coffee, gave the guests good cheer. And how they all did eat and call for a second and third helping! It was a cold, windy night, but the rude, dingy interior of our quarters, with a bright fire in the corner, and the candles and coal-oil lamps casting a warm and mellow glow over all, made every-

---

[25] Barboncito is not an uncommon Navajo name and it should not necessarily be assumed the reference here is to the famous Navajo leader of this period. See Lawrence C. Kelly, *Navajo Roundup, Selected Correspondence of Kit Carson's Expedition Against the Navajo, 1863–1865* (Boulder: The Pruett Publishing Company, [1970]), p. 145n.

one feel at home and conveyed the idea of much comfort and enjoyment.[26]

Alas! All are now dead and gone! Not one survives of that circle of Thanksgiving guests, save myself, on that never-to-be-forgotten day in far distant and long-since-abandoned Fort Wingate.

[26] The two most celebrated holidays in the military calendar were always the Fourth of July and Thanksgiving. For an interesting look at the same November 26, 1868, Thanksgiving celebration at another post also just opened, see the account of De B. Randolph Keim at Camp Supply, Indian Territory in *Sheridan's Troopers on the Borders: A Winter Campaign on the Plains* (Philadelphia: Claxton, Remsen and Haffelflinger, 1870), pp. 108–9.

A Troublesome Indian— Primping the Squaws

One day, after soothing and nursing my teething baby, I sat there alone while she lay in her cradle, fretful and crying. Largho, the old medicine man of the Indians, came in, and seating himself, asked what was the matter with the baby. I told him, whereupon he arose, and looking at her for a moment, gave a grunt of understanding and told me he could cure her.

Going outside he soon returned with a huge bunch of rattle-snake rattles in his hand. Seating himself by the cradle, he began to chant, meantime shaking the rattles ceaselessly, while I looked on in wonder and astonishment.

Sure enough! Soon the baby's cries grew fainter and fainter, until they finally ceased and she fell asleep. Now whether it was the droning incantations of the old medicine man or the medicines I had previously given her myself that brought about the desired effect, I cannot say.

However, old Largho was delighted with the success of his

experiment, and was more firmly convinced than ever of the efficacy of his skill and wonderful medicinal powers.

I was seldom left entirely alone in our house, for although the Indians had never as yet made any unfriendly demonstrations they were not always to be trusted, as at some fancied slight they might become insulting, especially toward a solitary woman.[27]

Barboncito came one day when I was alone, although my two neighbors' houses were so near I could reach out and touch their sides. He demanded whisky. I could see that he had been drinking, for there was always someone to surreptitiously give the Indians whisky. I told him I had none, but he refused to believe me. Pointing to a bottle standing on a shelf in the dining room he ordered me, with a threatening air, to go and bring it. As I knew he could not read the label, "Hostetters' Bitters," I told him to "help himself." He did so — with a huge pull, followed by a yell and a jump! I darted outside, and as fast as my feet could carry me, I rushed for the sutler's store and the little back room where the officers were lounging. For once this was a haven for me. Barboncito disappeared for some time, and then confined himself to a remote part of the reservation.

After this episode, more stringent methods were used to prevent any further trespassing by the Indians. They were very fond of music, and frequently would come to see me and ask me to play on the organ. I never refused their requests. Their delight was childish, and one huge Indian told me he would dance while I played. He told me he would come back, and he did so, arrayed in the costume of a beef hide, with the head and horns. The hide was a fresh one, right from a slaughtered animal, still wet and dripping blood. He took his stand without,

[27] Fort Wingate was near the Navajo Reservation as designated by the treaty of June 1868. The tribe was removed from their holding quarters at Fort Sumner, where they had been held since their roundup by Kit Carson four years previous, and brought to Wingate. They remained at the post for approximately five months while reservation boundaries were surveyed and agency buildings were prepared. See Ruth Underhill, *Here Come the Navaho!* (Lawrence: United States Indian Service, 1953), 183ff.

and I played, convulsed with laughter at the sight. A crowd of Indians had collected who were as much amused as myself. In the meantime and during the performance, I had sent word to the sutler's store of what was going on. A few soldiers and my alarmed husband soon appeared on the scene and dispersed the "star performer" as well as the crowd.

The squaws were curious and admiring as to various details of my toilet, especially as to my mode of wearing my hair and the method of producing the effect of the waves and crimps — then a fashionable style. One young squaw watched me arrange my hair with the crimping pins and clasps. I told her to come in the morning and see the effect. She did so, walking into my quarters before I was out of bed. I told her to watch while I combed my hair, and when she saw the locks of wavy tresses, her delight was unbounded. She wanted me to arrange her own hair in a similar manner, which I did. I sent to the sutler's store for some hairpins, and the toilet was soon made. It was quite unlike anything she had seen before. I told her not to comb her hair until the following morning. She appeared promptly, and when she saw the transformation of her straight locks into waves and curls, her admiration was beyond expression.

Away she went, but the next morning she brought several of her companions, and each and every one was treated likewise. Each assisted in adorning the other, and such an array of giggling, crimpheaded squaws had never before been seen in all the history of Fort Wingate. Feminine vanity and tastes are much the same the world over, no matter what the race or color.

I found my friendly, well-meant intentions had been an exceedingly tactful move, and bore good and fruitful results. During my life at Fort Wingate thereafter the Indian women were my firm friends, and rendered me various favors and kindnesses.

The cavalry officers stationed there had been old friends of my husband prior to his marriage, and extended their friendship to me naturally. All were bachelors with one exception, and all were ever welcome to our quarters. We made them as com-

fortable as we could, and administered to their appetites for the
"flesh pots of Egypt." Their bachelor mess was lacking in many
of the little dainties which they were given at our table. They
showed their appreciation in divers ways — gifts of game, etc.,
while every day one of their horses stood before my door for my
use and pleasure. I had my own sidesaddle and riding habit.
What had been lacking was a suitable mount, and this they
supplied.

As I look back through the vista of years, — so many, many
years ago — I can see only a vision of death. Oh, the many
graves with their sad array of former delightful, dauntless
cavalry officers! Some lived to attain distinction in after years,
but now, all are gone. Their memory, however, will never be
forgotten and their brave deeds will live after them.

The Indians were quiet and peaceable — no unfriendly
demonstrations — the issue of beef gave them something to live
on, which with what game they brought in kept them in food
most of the time. The fish they did not want, as they refused, for
some reason, to eat them, but were not averse to catching and
selling them to the garrison and civilians at the post.

Horseback rides and expeditions to not-far-distant or remote
surroundings were made by the officers and their ladies. Our
chief points of interest were at Agua Azula Springs, where trout
and other fish were to be found in quantities. When fried over
a hot fire, seasoned and well "buttered" over with bacon grease
— for no real butter was to be had — and with plenty of bread
and coffee, it was a meal all enjoyed. What mattered it if the
cream was all condensed milk — not the excellent evaporated
preparations of this day and age — and then sweetened with
muscovado sugar, we enjoyed it to the utmost.

No one was possessed with a fastidious appetite, and all ate
with a relish what was provided. There is no sauce like hunger,
increased by a horseback ride in the keen air of the mountains or
Plains. Occasionally these feasts by the roadside were further
varied by a stew or roast of bird or rabbit, all cooked together in
a Dutch oven.

On one of these trips we started with a detail of soldiers for
Fort Defiance, N. M. [Arizona Territory] forty miles northwest from Wingate. It had been abandoned a long time since,
but during its existence the Navajos had repeatedly besieged
and attacked the place. It had been guarded by troops while
the quarters and buildings were being erected. It was located
at the mouth of a canyon, with a dense growth of timber on the
hills surrounding it — a point of vantage for enemies, as they
were almost concealed in their approach.[28]

There were many legends and tales concerning the fort —
of torture, captivity and heroism of the men and officers. It was
a dismal spot, yet had once been busy with life and humanity.
The log houses had fallen into decay; the roofs were sagging and
open, and the interiors full of weeds and brush in which mice
and pack-rats scuttled about, their solitude undisturbed.

The Indians avoided the place, remembering the many tales
that had been broadcast about it, and so we found the ruins
silent and desolate. Behind the fort, and in proximity to it, was
the cemetery. Wooden headboards or markers bore the names
of the quiet sleepers beneath. The weather and storms of years
had almost obliterated them, while the melancholy spot was
overgrown with a jungle of deadly nightshade, wild vines and
a rank growth of weeds.

We did not linger long around the ruins of old Fort Defiance. We had seen enough of its desolation, and the history of
the old post was so replete with disaster and death that its
memory was full of sadness. Even at this late day I cannot
forget the impression it made upon me. I was glad to reach my
own squalid adobe quarters at Fort Wingate, with its lack of
conveniences, its dirt floor covered over with hay, and the ingrain carpet stretched over all; with the bright fire, the crowing

---

[28] Fort Defiance, the first United States Army post in what is now Ari-
zona, was established at the mouth of Canyon Bonito in 1851 to control
the Navajo Indians. It was abandoned ten years later and the garrison
removed to Fort Fauntleroy which was the forerunner of Fort Lyons. Fort
Defiance became the site of the Navajo Indian Agency in 1868 and remains
so today.

baby, and the ever-faithful striker in the kitchen broiling a
steak. It seemed like Paradise to me after what we had just
beheld. It was HOME, after all, and no tragedy or disaster had
as yet happened within its walls. My soldier and I were young
— and we were living!

Returning East—
Hardships and
Difficulties En Route

Our garrison shortly after was saddened by the sudden death, January 3, 1869, of one of the cavalry officers, Captain J. R. Kemball [Kemble], Third Cavalry. It was the first fatality to occur after our arrival from Old Fort Wingate, and his funeral greatly depressed us. He was interred with every honor due his rank, until such time as arrangements could be made with his relatives in the East regarding the transportation of his body thither. His wife and daughter, who had been with him while we were stationed at Old Wingate, had returned home when the troops were sent to our present location, so he was deprived of their comfort when death came.

We received news that, much to our regret and against our desires, it would be necessary for me to go to my home in the East. As it was impossible for my husband to accompany me at that time, I would be obliged to travel alone unless fortunate enough to have a companion. The weather was severe and stormy and the journey would be rough and comfortless, for there were no stages or railroads to ensure speed and comfort until the terminus of the Kansas Pacific railroad was reached, which at that time was at Sheridan, Kansas, more than a thousand miles distant. The entire distance to the railroad had to be traveled in stages and ambulance.

Most fortunately for me, Mr. [Waters], a post trader and a partner of the post trader at Wingate, was going to Fort Leavenworth, Kansas, and offered his help and services in any way possible. We were only too glad to avail ourselves of his kindness, and thankfully accepted his offer. He had always appeared to be a pleasant and agreeable gentleman, and his wife was an acquaintance of ours.

So we departed in as comfortable a manner as possible, our ambulance filled with robes and blankets, a footstove to warm our feet, and plenty of pillows and cushions.

We reached Santa Fe without accident, where, after a rest of twenty-four hours, we sent the ambulance back to the post, took the stage and resumed our journey. The conveyance was a Concord coach, with a seating capacity of twelve persons, and often more, with a little crowding. The springs were of leather, which greatly facilitated the ease of locomotion over rough roads.

But alas! A sudden change of temper came over the erstwhile agreeable and solicitous Mr. [Waters]. He was now surly and irritable, and paid no attention to me or my baby, but slept most of the time, and vented his whisky-scented breath in loud snores, greatly to my disgust and not a little uneasiness. The driver saw how circumstances were, and told me not to be alarmed. He took the precaution, however, to remove the trader's revolver.

In course of time we reached Bent's Fort, or, as originally known, Old Fort Bent or Fort William (named for William Bent). It had been built by the trading firm of Bent & St. Vrain, designed to be used as a trading post. Many vicissitudes had this famous stronghold gone through since it was established so many years before. It had passed through prosperity, waning fortune and finally entire destruction, and at the time of my arrival there was nothing remaining to the old post but mounds of adobe.[29] Men whose names had been a power on the far-off frontier, whose wealth and influence and adventures made them famous in the history of the West, were linked with Bent's Fort.

The present Fort Bent [Lyon] was a comfortable and almost rural scene of peace and quiet, with horses and cattle grazing in the pastures and on the adjoining prairie.

Descending from the stage coach we thankfully entered the building and were made welcome by the head of the house, a big man garbed in true western style — breeches reinforced with buckskin, and wearing boots, spurs, and of course a gun and bowie knife in his belt. He introduced me to his mother, a tiny, sweet old lady, who seemed to me almost like an angelic vision in contrast to the usual females I had met in my travels.

The supper was soon ready, the table with napery and glass and a centerpiece of pine cones in graduated size, beautiful and unique, which was in strange contrast to the tin cups and thick stone earthenware prevalent at the stage stations on the route. But what was this? Surely my eyes deceived me! A plate of real sour-cream biscuit, with preserves and home-made cake! Verily, it was a feast fit for the gods.

There had been rumors and reports of Indian hostilities among the various tribes infesting the stage route, in scattering bands between Santa Fe and Sheridan, the railroad terminus. The ranchmen and others and Bent's Fort had armed themselves in readiness to resist attacks. Guards were posted nightly about the place, while a sergeant and a detail of four soldiers, at the request of the ranchmen to the commanding officer of the nearest military post, had been sent to them to assist in their protection.

[29] In about 1829 William and Charles Bent built their trading post on the Arkansas River near the present La Junta, Colorado. Twenty years later this post was dismantled and Bent's new fort was established in time to be sold to the War Department and renamed Fort Fauntleroy, Fort Wise, and finally Fort Lyon. It was abandoned by the military in June 1867 and a new Fort Lyon was constructed.

Naturally my alarm was not allayed when the following morning we made ready to resume our journey. I heard the sergeant giving his orders to his men to "Keep your eyes peeled and be ready to give them Injuns hell if they show up." He "Reckoned that lady will yell like hell if we're attacked."

With a hearty hand-grasp and goodby to the sweet chatelaine of Bent's Fort, I climbed within the yawning old Concord. The curtains had been pulled down, and it was with a sinking heart that I took my seat with six male passengers. Apparently divining my fears, a voice in the darkened interior assured me that there was no danger, either from Indians or themselves; so the driver, with a whoop and crack of his whip, started away, the sergeant and two soldiers riding in front and the other two in the rear, as guards and escort.

Nothing occurred to alarm me. The roads were unobstructed and smooth, the passengers considerate and kind as to my comfort and that of my baby, which they took turns in holding, this greatly relieving my tired back. Each offered to hold her when we stopped for dinner at a lonely hut.

Never in all my experience on the frontier, varied and strange as it has been, have I met with more spontaneous and ready kindness than from these uncouth, roughly-garbed and warm-hearted men of the Plains, in some instances outcasts and outlaws as well.

It was late in the afternoon of a cold and stormy day when we drove up to the "Hotel Perry" at Sheridan. Mr. [Waters] gathered himself together, restored to his sane and natural self. He apologized to me for his "indiscreetness," as he indulgently called it, and attributed it to an attack of a disease with which he was afflicted, and added, with further assurances, that he would attend to my baggage and check it to my final destination.

It was an exhausted and benumbed woman who sought shelter and warmth in the parlors of the Hotel Perry. What a vision of cozy comfort it seemed, with its ingrain carpet, the huge base burner stove diffusing warmth and cheer, the chromos on the papered wall,[30] together with a hair wreath under glass, with a companion piece composed of watermelon and muskmelon seeds. There were photographs of western celebrities, books and old newspapers on the marble-topped stand; also a perforated cardboard motto, wrought in worsted, with the motto, "God Bless Our Home," hanging over the door.

All this combined to increase my spirit of thankfulness that I was out of the Concord coach, free at least from the ceaseless rumble of wheels, the cracking of whips and the shouts of the drivers, which had been dinned into my ears for days. Mr. Perry, the landlord, soon appeared, and ringing a bell announced supper. He conducted me to a bare and draughty dining room. I did not see Mrs. Perry.

After supper, and as soon as possible, I was shown to my room, a small corner apartment overlooking the wind-swept prairie. It was furnished with a cot and insufficient bedding, and a mattress too thin to induce slumber, as the slats were quite in evidence. The floor was bare and devoid of covering, as were the pillows. The snow had blown through the small, curtainless window and formed little mounds on the sill, and drifted softly but surely onto the bed from the unplastered ceiling. To my wretched discomfort, the baby, wrapped in every article available, lifted up her voice in misery. In the midst of her lamentations, a voice thundered forth from an adjoining room, "Can't you choke that brat!" I went down stairs to the parlor where I could at least keep warm, I thought; but attempting to open the door I was prevented by some obstacle. This proved to be a sleeping guest on the floor, while others lay about the room in all sorts of positions. The hotel was crowded, beds all taken, and the parlor had been utilized as well to accommodate the overflow.

However, I managed to squeeze my way in and over the disturbed sleeper, who demanded to know, "What in hell I was doing there?" I endeavored, in a faltering voice, to explain,

---

[30] Chromolithographing is simply lithographing in color.

whereupon hearing me, and beholding the baby, he arose and secured a chair for me, made room beside the stove, where I remained for the rest of the night, half-dozing, with the comforted baby sleeping on the blanket which the repentant men insisted that I make use of.

When it was broad daylight, the various sleepers aroused and disappeared, while I, considerably refreshed by the genial warmth of the room and what little slumber I had been able to snatch, arose from my chair and made my way to the kitchen, guided by sounds of rattling pans and the smell of frying meat. Within I heard the voice of an angry woman.

Timid and doubtful, I opened the door and beheld Mrs. Perry, a worn-out, tired-looking woman, busily engaged in preparing breakfast. Mr. Perry was a meek and subdued heap in one corner, evidently the object of his wife's wrath, the cause being — so I was informed — overindulgence in the cup that cheers. I politely explained my plight of the previous night, and asked permission to remain in the kitchen until breakfast was ready, as there was as yet no fire in the parlor stove, after which I would resume my journey and trouble her no further. There was no cordiality in her invitation to take a seat on the hewn end of a stump serving as a seat behind the stove, which I did, and as far as possible away from it, so as not to be in the way of her wrath myself.[31]

Finally something must have awakened her pity, for she looked at the baby in its forlorn mother's arms, relented in her lack of kindly greeting and took the baby from me, holding it with one arm while she continued her cooking of ham and eggs. Meantime she adjured the stupid Mr. Perry to either give the lady the only chair there was or get out, as he was making more trouble than he was worth. She apologized for this little "family scene," and explained the situation. Mr. Perry had been

[31] In a later meeting Alice described Mrs. Perry as "a mean, ill-tempered old vixen. We none of us like any of them nor no one else in town that knows them." Alice Baldwin to Frank Baldwin, October 1, 1869, Baldwin Collection, Box 7.

drunk, more or less, for a week, and had neglected household affairs and business in general, leaving the management of the entire house, as well as outdoor matters, to his wife. She said she was discouraged and had made up her mind to endure it no longer unless her husband turned over a new leaf.

Mr. Perry must have "reformed," for eventually the Hotel Perry became a popular hostelry for tourists and travelers from all over the world.

Arrival at Hays City —
A Night of Sleepless Horror

In due course of time we arrived at Hays City — a typical specimen of the frontier towns of that day, scattered at intervals along the lines of the railroad, affording at best scant comfort and rest to the traveler.

The usual one wide thoroughfare prevailed at Hays, with its square-faced, flat-roofed houses bordering on either side, extending through the entire length of the "city."

In proximity to each other, regardless of business pursuits, were to be found the one "millinery and dressmaking establishment," next door to "Mike's Place," and he in turn to a butcher shop, contiguous to a pig pen — considerately placed somewhat in the rear, just off from the prairie which closely skirted the town.

Dance parlors were numerous, with many saloons, while concert halls cordially invited any stranger within the gates of Hays City to enter and be refreshed. It was a heterogeneous populace — cowboys drunk and shooting up the town; soldiers on leave for a day; a few blanketed Indians, silent, sullen and

KANSAS STATE HISTORICAL SOCIETY, TOPEKA

Hays City, central Kansas, in 1868. Founded in 1867 near Fort Hays,
a military post from 1865 to 1889, it was incorporated as a city in 1885.

observing, with an occasional "tenderfoot" in eastern store
clothes, giving a fine contrast to the western attire of his
companions.

In surveying the shifting, polyglot scene I was reminded of
the quotation of "mongrel puppy, whelp and hound, and cur of
low degree."

Conspicuous on the street was the one hotel of the town.
I do not now recall the name of the proprietor, but I do remember the giant negro porter, who seemed to me to be the embodi-
ment of strength. Never before had I beheld such an evil face,
and it turned out a fitting individuality for the night of horror
that took place during the interval I was obliged to spend there.

Mr. [Waters] had disappeared—apparently forever, despite
his previous apologies and promises, and I never saw him again.
I was shown to my room — a small, bare one, containing a
single cot and one chair, with no other conveniences whatever.
The partition between my room and the adjoining one reached
a little more than half way to the ceiling. There was a knothole
just about in the center of the partition. Naturally I was desirous

of as much privacy as possible from any activities of a "Peeping Tom" on the other side of the partition, and judging from the voices and clink of glasses there were several men in the room.

So I fastened my shawl over the knothole, using a pin to hold it in place, and made ready for sleep and as much rest as possible on the uninviting bed. The pillow was an old salt bag stuffed with straw.

The big porter had conducted me to my "chamber of horrors," and deposited my traveling bag on the chair. He advised me to place it close against the door, which opened out upon a passageway. The lock in the door was useless and consequently my door could not be fastened in any manner from the inside.

I finally crawled into bed and lay there shivering and striving to find a place in the hard mattress without lumps. I kept my eye on that knothole, and, as I expected, some man on the other side presently "got busy." I saw the shawl over the knothole move, and it was slowly poked aside. That was too much for my Irish blood. I hurled one of my shoes at the hole, and it struck the partition with a bang!

After that there was a brief lull of sounds and voices on the other side. But after a time out broke a racket in the hallway. Presently came the roar of guns, loud yells and much scuffling. Suddenly my door crashed in, carrying with it the huge negro porter, who fell dead on the floor of my room!

He had warned me not to be afraid, as he would be on guard all night. He was a discharged soldier of the Tenth Cavalry, and was standing up close against the door when shot, the frail woodwork giving way to his huge bulk.

Throughout all this fracas the baby slept peacefully. Needless to say there was no sleep for me, so I arose and dressed and waited for the dawn, which was soon breaking. The wife of the landlord told me she had locked herself in her room, as shooting scrapes were common, but that she never could get used to them.

The remainder of this never-to-be-forgotten journey to Chicago was uneventful enough. We were nearing civilization, in fact, were in it. Farms, vineyards and cities began to appear. Gone were the experiences and dangers of the far wild frontier.

The joyful arrival at home, the reunion of life-long friends, the privileges and advantages of eastern life, made the past three years seem like a century.

While enjoying my visit home I received a telegram from my husband. He had been ordered from Fort Wingate to join his regiment, then stationed at Fort Hays, Kansas. Brevet Brigadier General [Nelson A.] Miles was its colonel and then in command at Fort Leavenworth.

This meant that my visit must be at once terminated, so bidding all goodby I joined my husband at Fort Hays.

The next few years saw us successively at Fort Harker, then at Detroit (on recruiting duty), then with the regiment again at Newport Barracks, Kentucky, and from there to Fort Leavenworth, Kansas. Whilst at this last post in 1876 the horrible news of the Custer Massacre reached us.

It was but a few hours before preparations for the departure of the Fifth Infantry for the front were made without delay, under the supervision of experienced officers. Crowds of people from the city and vicinity came to watch the assembling soldiery and all was excitement and anticipation.

Finally the day of departure came. The chartered special train stood puffing and steaming on the track. The hour had come for farewells and tears from the wives and sweethearts of the departing troops. The train was packed with soldiers within and without, on the roofs of the coaches and hanging to straps to catch the last glimpse of the dear ones left behind. To the strains from the band of "The Girl I Left Behind Me," the train pulled out, and that was the last farewell for many a brave soldier.

It was a desolate and forlorn Fort Leavenworth after the troops had left. The long-abandoned fife and drum now gave the summons for duty. The summer was naturally a quiet and

melancholy one. Disease afflicted various families at the post
with fatal results, carrying sadness everywhere.

However, this was somewhat relieved by the arrival of two
batteries of the Third Artillery as reinforcements to fill the
vacancy caused by the departed troops. Several companies of
the Twenty-Third Infantry also came. The influx of so many
people, together with the few remaining officers and their families of the Fifth Infantry, necessitated the doubling up of families to provide quarters for all. The old saying that no house is
large enough for two families to dwell in harmony, was not true
in this enforced arrangement, for so far as I know and remember, peace and harmony reigned everywhere; there was no
alternative. We made the best of conditions and formed lasting
friendships.

In early spring, 1877, after a tedious winter, the few remaining officers, quartermaster and commissary, and the ladies of the
regiment, went by boat up the Missouri to join their husbands
in the wild wastes of the frontier. I went in advance of the
others, in order to make a visit with relatives at Sioux City,
Iowa, this city being en route to my final destination.

I was obliged to wait several weeks for a river steamboat to
arrive at Sioux City. The "Silver City" was a comfortable boat
with ample staterooms and was clean and convenient. There
were quite a number of passengers, and a cosmopolitan lot they
certainly were, all, however, being civil and pleasant. The wife
of the captain and a few other ladies, myself included, made an
agreeable circle of our own. There were professional gamblers
on board who nightly fleeced many of the men. There was also
a variety troupe who embarked at a little wayside station a few
days after we left Sioux City. They gave several performances
of songs and dances that were quite creditable and certainly
diverting to say the least, all in good humor and desirous of
pleasing the passengers.

The paymaster, Major [George] Candee, with his clerks
and escort of soldiers, well armed, came on board, and to my

surprise and pleasure I found he was going to Fort Keogh, my
own destination.[32] And so we journeyed up the broad Missouri
toward the far western frontier.

[32] In June of 1877 when Alice and Juanita were taking passage up the
Missouri River, the post eventually to be named Fort Keogh (in November
1878) was called Cantonment on Tongue River. Alice and Nita were met
at Fort Buford on June 6 and completed the journey to the cantonment
with Frank. Baldwin Diary (1877).

Life on the Steamboat — Missouri River Travel

One day an air of suppressed excitement seemed to prevail aboard. The captain and his boat officials held whispered conclaves with the paymaster outside on the deck, apart from the other passengers. They conversed in low tones, or ceased entirely at the approach of anyone. The gamblers and cowboys and men in general were evidently on the alert for something out of the ordinary to occur, as they examined their pistols and revolvers, and were seen to be scanning the surrounding country and every wood landing that the steamer approached. Even the roustabouts below were watchful, crowding to the edge of the boat and looking, either keeping silent or talking among themselves.

But what was the mystery? The women, as was their wont, were inclined to be frightened and apprehensive when not taken into confidence in the face of impending danger. The wife of the captain asked him what was the trouble. He did not tell her, but made an evasive answer, which only served to increase our anxiety. It eventually developed that the paymaster had heard that he was to be attacked by road agents at a certain point along the river, and robbed. They knew he had a considerable sum of money in his possession for the troops. He had explained the situation to the captain of the boat, who, in turn, had apprised the male passengers to be on their guard and all ready for the expected attack. Fortunately nothing happened, and we proceeded on our way with no further fear or disturbance.

Below decks dwelt "Fannie," a good-sized pig, but of tender age. She had been rescued from a passing steamboat when she fell into the river, and was hauled aboard by one of the roustabouts of the "Silver City" who saw her floundering in the water. She had become a pet with the crew and ventured on familiarities among the passengers, which were not encouraged. One morning while at breakfast in the saloon, who should appear but Fannie, clambering up the stairs that led from the lower deck, the saloon being the first objective point, especially at meal time, and Fannie knew as well as anyone when to come, although probably the appetizing odors attracted her. To my amusement and my little daughter's delight and under the protective cover of a good-natured male passenger who sat next to us, Fannie was fed and filled with many a slyly handed biscuit and tidbit from the table, until the unsympathetic steward discovered and routed Fannie to her rightful quarters below decks.

Life on board the "Silver City" was quiet and uneventful, save for the stops along the river at various landing places to "wood up," when a little diversion was enjoyed in watching the crew go ashore. The boat would crowd as closely as practicable to the river bank, the gangplank would be thrown out for the crew, also for Fannie, who would forage and grunt and wander about seeking whatever she could find in the eatable line. After the wood had all been carried aboard, the whistle would sound as a signal of departure, when Fannie, aroused by the sound, would come clattering across the gangplank, sometimes a little late on her return, but no matter how far she had wandered away the boat always waited for her to return before proceeding.

The cuisine of the steamer was excellent, while the cook himself never failed in his preparations for each and every dish. His hot rolls and pastries and roasts were not to be surpassed, the coffee was delicious and the ice cream served on Sundays was beyond criticism, even though made from condensed milk. I gave it as my opinion that a cook as skilled in his profession must have a clean and orderly kitchen, and I insisted that I would like to peep into it. I did — and what I beheld made me wish I had not, and convinced me that we cannot always judge from appearances! I laughingly told the captain of my experience, and he remarked that you "never could tell from the size of a toad how far he could jump."

That same evening I saw the cook come out from his hot, cell-like kitchen, wiping his perspiring face with a dish towel! Evidently he believed in being clean — even at the expense of the towel he used on our table dishes!

One day we were hailed by a man from the bank of the river. As the boat pulled up in answer to his hail, we saw he was a tall, hale, fine-looking man in the uniform of a cavalryman. He proved to be Captain Gustavus Doane of the Second Cavalry. He had with him a detachment of Crow Indians and their families, who were being conveyed to another part of the territory. Among the squaws was one young woman in whom I was particularly interested. She had a delicate, refined face, and her general appearance was above the average among Indian women. Her English was grammatically correct. I was astonished to see her among the crude and simple squaws. She told me she had been educated at a Catholic school, and was then on her way to the Crow Agency, as were the rest of the Indians. I was much impressed, and have since wondered what was her ultimate fate.

While Captain Doane and the male members of the party were talking, I went around in the encampment and tents of the women. They were filled with wonder as to my attire, and urged by their innocent, and I must confess, feminine curiosity, I consented to undress and let them see for themselves. They crowded around me. Crinoline and corsets they marveled at, but did not admire. Through the interpreter, Mary, the pretty squaw previously mentioned, they said they did not see how I could wear so many clothes, and wished to know if I did not suffer from the heat and exhaustion when the weather was hot. Details of other articles elicited favorable criticism, and met with their approval as to their use and protection when the weather was cold. My hair, arranged in the fashionable coiffure of the day, they were delighted with, and insisted that I take it down so they could see how much of it was mine. One ancient Crow woman, taking a strand in her hand, examined it carefully, and said she thought I had a scalp in my tresses. At this point Mary whispered something to her, and no more was said on the subject.

The voices of Indian women are naturally soft and melodious, and as I sat or stood among them, listening to their chatter and laughter, and no doubt passing uncomplimentary comments about me, I felt that it all meant sincerity, which does not always prevail in a cultured and fashionable society.

Our delay and visit occupied much of the afternoon, and it was the hour of dinner. Captain Doane accepted the invitation of the boat captain to dine with us. It was evident that it had been a great pleasure to meet with us and to mingle and converse with people of his own race again after so much solitude and desolation, living among a crude and alien people. Such a life is not conducive to happiness or peace of mind.[33]

In the due course of time we arrived at Fort Abraham Lincoln, opposite the city of Bismarck. It was just about time for "retreat" as the bugles were blowing and the drums beating. All were quiet and saddened by the memory of the passing of that heroic regiment, the Seventh Cavalry, General [George] Custer's regiment, which had marched away from this post but

[33] The episode involving Captain Doane and his relocating Crow Indians seems not to have occurred on Alice's trip up the Missouri in June but rather was an event that happened at the Yellowstone and Big Horn rivers on July 4 and 5, 1877, when she and Nita accompanied Frank on routine duty on the steamer *Rankin*. Baldwin Diary (1877).

a few brief weeks before.[34] The officers' quarters and the men's barracks loomed against the sunset sky, empty and silent. Few occupants were at the post, which once thrilled to music and glittering parade. Not even the barking of dogs was to be heard, or the shouts of children. The sorrow-burdened women were all gone, and this noted post seemed desolate and forlorn.

As we reflected on what had been so tragic, our sadness was increased by the news of the sinking of the steamboat, "Don Cameron," which was conveying the ladies of the Fifth Infantry and the few remaining officers left behind at the departure of the regiment some months before. A total loss of baggage and property was the result. Fortunately no lives were lost. A snag had pierced the hull of the steamer. Another boat, just ahead, at once turned about and came to the rescue of her mate. Scenes of confusion followed, and many amusing incidents occurred — one in particular I well recall.

A staunch and valorous Irishman named Roach, the regimental quartermaster's henchman, had persuaded the quartermaster that he be allowed to bring along his cow, "with th' rist av th' regiment," as he expressed it. When the boat started to sink Roach grabbed the cow by the tail and hung on "like grim death to a nigger." The cow refused to be driven to a place of safety; she bellowed with terror. Time was short and something had to be done at once. The shouts of the excited passengers maddened the poor brute and transformed her from a peaceable and mellow bovine into a frantic, lunging creature. She turned her lowered horns into the desperate Roach and sent him overboard into the river, still pursued by the maddened cow! Here both floundered about until Roach clambered onto her back and endeavored to ride the animal ashore! It was all in vain, however; so Roach slid off, grabbed her by the tail and, amid the shouts and laughter of the passengers, was thus towed to safety, swearing a blue streak meantime.

[34] This statement by Alice Baldwin is a little confusing. General George Custer and the Seventh Cavalry were massacred at the Little Big Horn the year before (June 25, 1876). Alice must be referring to the departure of the remnants of the regiment leaving for duty elsewhere "a few brief weeks before."

The Tongue River
Cantonment —
The Nez Perce Uprising

The Indian Territory Expedition was carried on to a successful and victorious close, followed by the surrender of Chief Joseph of the Nez Perces.[35] The subjugation of lesser chiefs made a condition of comparative peace and security.

Battalions of the Eighteenth, Twenty-Second, and First Infantry and a troop of the Seventh Cavalry, all commanded by experienced officers, made the entire command all the more satisfied as to their safety in general. The cantonment on Tongue River, afterwards named Fort Keogh, was, as might be imagined, a collection of log houses, built of not more than two rooms each. The logs were placed perpendicularly in the ground and the chinks and crannies filled with mud, which served to keep

[35] Without thinking, Alice confused the Indian Territory Expedition of 1874–75, which took place in Texas and Indian Territory on the Southern Great Plains, with the Sioux War of 1876–77 recently stalemated on the Northern Plains. Chief Joseph's eleven-week retreat of the Nez Perce concluded October 6, 1877, at the Bear Paws Battle Ground, Montana.

out the wind and rain until, as time went on and the unseasoned timbers shrunk and the "chinking" fell out, it was necessary to "replaster" it.

The ladies of the regiment had all arrived, and homes and family circles were once more established. There were many young bachelor officers among the different encampments who were eager enough, after months of hard field service, to avail themselves of every social activity and pleasurable enjoyment.

The steamer "Far West," probably the most historic craft that ever plied the waters of the Missouri River, with its noted commander, Captain Grant Marsh, had brought a distinguished party of guests to inspect the cantonment and to see the wild and primitive country. The arrival of General [William T.] Sherman with his staff officers and acquaintances, made life a round of diversion and duty.[36] There were parades, guard mount and drills by the troops, both cavalry and infantry, all of

[36] General Sherman, commander of the United States Army, visited the cantonment on July 17, 1877.

MONTANA HISTORICAL SOCIETY, HELENA

Fort Keogh, Montana, ca 1879. Established in 1876 as a base of supply and operations against the Sioux Indians, it was originally called Cantonment on Tongue River. The post was named Fort Keogh in November 1878.

which made a most interesting spectacle before the keen eye of
the famous general. If any mistakes or errors were made in any
of the evolutions, it was not discerned by the innocent and un-
practiced tourists.

Captain Marsh placed his steamboat at the service of the
command, and as the band of the Fifth Infantry was along to
furnish music, we danced and made merry until reveille with the
"Virginia Reel," "Money Musk" and "Varsouviana," with heel
and toe, polka and mazurka. The always popular schottische
was also not neglected, while all whirled through the mazes of
the quadrille and cotillion. It was "On with the dance, let joy
be unconfined" and it continued until the warning notes of
"Home Sweet Home" broke up the festivities. Truly it was the
essence of enjoyment. The remoteness of the cantonment; the
novelty of everything! What mattered it to the gallant warriors
on board, the lack of evening dress? They wore their campaign
rigging of trousers reinforced with buckskin, their bespurred
heels jingling and making occasional rents in the gowns of the
ladies!

The spring and summer following were strenuous and excit-
ing ones, varied by forays and preparations for the forthcom-
ing permanent quarters for officers and barracks for the troops,
and the erection of stables for the horses. All this kept everyone busy.

The genial sutler, Mr. William D. O'Toole, himself a West
Pointer but resigned from the service by his own inclinations,
was an enterprising and agreeable factor in the united and combined activities of the cantonment. His lovely wife was an
efficient aid in all her husband's plans and efforts to promote
pleasures and social life. During a dull period, when days
dragged in dreary monotony, all made the best of everything,
and good humor prevailed; but this lull was only short-lived
after all.

Rumors of uprisings among the Indians were rife, with
threatened attacks. Chief Joseph and his band of Nez Perces
were on the warpath. Preparations were at once made to take

the field.[37] Consternation prevailed among the ladies and not a few tears were shed, many of them never before having had any experiences in Indian war alarms, and naturally there was much apprehension regarding their men-folks. However, this did not prevent them from meeting the threatened danger with composure when the hour of departure drew near.

Lizzie Sherman, the one and lovely young belle of the garrison lamented, "What a change in the spirit of our dreams," while giving an encore before the departing braves as she waved in either hand a tiny American flag, the beautiful girl herself standing beneath Old Glory which waved above the commander's quarters. She was of a stock and breed to do and dare, despite her feminine fears.

The evening before it was the Sabbath. We had all gathered in our little log drawing room to say goodby. I had in my keeping a piano, waiting for its owner to arrive later. We played and sang "Sweet By and By," "On the Other Side of Jordan," and other good old hymns of the Long Ago. When Captain Owen Hale, Seventh Cavalry, bold, dashing, dauntless trooper that he was, sang "And just beyond the shining shore I can almost discover," and I expressed my surprise at his familiarity with that good old song, he replied, "Mrs. Baldwin, I had a dear Methodist mother and was brought up on such hymns, and I wonder if I ever will forget them."

He was ever of a gay and cheerful temperament; but on this particular evening he seemed quiet and depressed. His last words to me, as he took my hand and bade me and the others goodby, were "Pray for me, for I am never coming back!" He never did! When Lieutenant George W. Baird, Fifth Infantry in the memorable fight at Bear Paw Mountain, in 1877, issued an order to Captain Hale and received no response, he approached and repeated the order to the yet silent captain. He

[37] Miles received an urgent dispatch on September 17, 1877, from General O. O. Howard requesting assistance. Troops were put into motion that very evening and marched to the north and west the following morning. Baldwin Diary (1877).

found him dead, his rifle in his hand, and kneeling as if taking aim. He had rested his carbine on top of a rock and in that position was struck and instantly killed, remaining there until found. Lieutenant J. W. Biddle of the Seventh Cavalry was killed in the same fight and lay close by his brother comrade in arms.[38] Thus died two brave and gallant men. Our infantry loss was great, one result being the severe wounding of Lieutenant Baird. One arm was shattered and the lower lobe of his left ear shot away. Captain Henry Romeyn was shot through the body and never recovered his strength, and was eventually retired.

That was a summer fraught with alternate changes of excitement and never-ceasing anxieties, and of course attended with the always-occurring deaths and disasters incident to warfare. It was at the battle of Wolf Mountain where my husband carried a load of ammunition on the front of his saddle up a steep hill to a line of soldiers fighting desperately against Sioux and Cheyenne warriors, without casting a thought regarding his own personal safety. He never slackened rein until his goal was reached, and then waving his cap to the advancing men he shouted, "Come on, men; follow me." And they obeyed orders "you bet!" as John Brughier, a half-breed interpreter, emphatically remarked, in describing the incident on his arrival several hours later, after the return of the victorious band of friendly Cheyenne and Sioux warriors against the Nez Perces three days prior to Brughier's arrival.[39]

[38] Captain Hale is reported to have responded to Miles's order to charge the Nez Perce camp at Snake Creek on the Bear Paws Battle Ground with the comment "My God, have I got to go out and get killed in such cold weather." Like his fellow officer, Second Lieutenant Jonathan W. Biddle, who had entered the service but one year and one month earlier, Hale died on September 30, 1877. See Merrill D. Beal, *"I Will Fight No More Forever," Chief Joseph and the Nez Perce War* (Seattle: University of Washington Press, 1966), pp. 215–16.

[39] Alice is confused in her chronology here for the Battle of Wolf Mountain, Montana, occurred on January 8, 1877, nearly ten months prior to the closing of the Nez Perce campaign. It is true that Frank was brave in his actions on Wolf Mountain for he was later made a brevet major for his conspicuous gallantry.

Those three days were agonizing to me and to the waiting women of the garrison, who were in anxious suspense for further news of the results of the battle. The "friendlies" who had come in to the garrison explained by signs that two of our officers were dead — but who? Thus each waiting heart questioned! When it was finally known that they were Comrades Hale and Biddle what grief and tears followed! What a scene of excitement was that day presented to the mud-bedaubed cantonment of log huts! Women seeking to encourage and comfort each other, while the few men at the cantonment — officers who had been detailed to remain behind instead of accompanying the expedition, to safeguard and protect both garrison and stores — affected a composure which they did not really feel, as they sought to console and cheer those inclined toward hysterics.

The scout, Brughier, surveyed the weeping ones with compassion and remarked, "I suppose God Almighty made them that way, but I don't know what for." This well known frontier character had married a squaw — he had the decent courage to marry her legally — and they had a brood of children that were an example for many a white child born to civilized and continued advantages of Christian precept and example. Johnny Brughier was illiterate, rough-and-ready, but he was the soul of honor and ever ready to do his duty wherever the situation placed him and required his best services.[40]

When at last the news arrived that the troops were in sight, coming over the bluffs across the Yellowstone, we all rushed out to greet the victors — some in ambulances, others in wheeled vehicles of every description, but most of us on horseback, men, women and children, with a following of dogs, barking and yelping. We galloped at top speed over the prairie and down

[40] Johnny Brugier or Bruguier was a twenty-eight-year-old fugitive from a murder charge at Standing Rock who joined Sitting Bull's forces after the Custer massacre. Miles lured him into army employ as a messenger and interpreter by promising to do what he could to clear the outstanding warrant. The scout was tried for murder in United States District Court at Fargo, and, with the favorable testimony of both Miles and Frank Baldwin, was acquitted December 31, 1879.

to the ferry, the Fifth Infantry band at the head of this polyglot procession, playing inspiring and martial airs which floated out and echoed among the bluffs and over the vast and silent plains and never ceased until the victors and vanquished had landed at the ferry and stepped off the boat with the illustrious but defeated Chief Joseph in their midst. He bore himself with a dignity and grace befitting a warrior of any race. His face wore an inscrutable look. He was a prisoner; he had lost in his fight for liberty and inherited rights which he and his race had possessed for years. He had lost all. The great chief was not at all impressed by the curious and staring spectators, nor even when the band struck up the old-time air, "No, No, Not for Joseph." The interpreter explained the hidden and tuneful satire of the song, but silently Joseph wrapped his blanket about him and said not a word. To the fallen chief it was like the bitterness of death. When he surrendered to General Miles, he cast a look upward as if apostrophizing the Great Spirit, and exclaimed, "From where the sun now sets I will fight the white man no more forever!" — words which have gone down in history. Chief Joseph was a wonderful Indian, and I doubt if his equal among them ever lived.[41]

[41] The correct quotation is "From where the sun now stands, I will fight no more forever." According to the surrender terms the Nez Perce were to be given winter quarters at Fort Keogh and then returned to their homeland in Idaho the following spring. These terms, however, were countermanded in the nation's capital and the tribesmen were banished to an unfamiliar reservation in Indian Territory. With the aid of Miles the Nez Perce were finally redeemed and allowed to return to the Pacific Northwest in May of 1885. Chief Joseph died on September 21, 1904, after a graceful old age in which he was regarded as a celebrity. See Beal, *"I Will Fight No More Forever,"* pp. 264–301.

An Adventure
In Cake-Making—
Another on Horseback

During the summer and after the foregoing campaign was concluded, we — the few remaining occupants of the garrison — led a peaceful and uneventful life. Anything which afforded a change or that would break the monotony, was welcomed.

So it happened one day, when I, like the others, had grown weary of the quietude of affairs, I concluded to make an attempt to bake a cake. Not all the necessary ingredients were at hand; but as with the Thanksgiving mince meat, I demonstrated again the motherly qualities of necessity.

I had previously put to soak some desiccated eggs — something I had not before tried in my culinary operations. The alluring label of "Directions" set forth on the can assured the victim-to-be that most satisfying results would follow if the instructions were carefully noted.

Determined to "do or die," I began operations. The desiccated eggs looked like pale yellow rock salt in the bulk. I made ready for the cake baking, arranging my various ingredients on the table in my tent, which was used for a dining room. This tent was located between two others, one used as a "front room" and the other as a kitchen. In the latter slept Kennedy, a faithful factotum of former years.[42]

Callers dropped in as I was working, among them three officers on duty at the garrison while their comrades were out on field service. They arranged themselves quietly and with no other announcement than that they were just making an informal call; but when some of my lady neighbors also dropped in, I asked them what their intentions were, whereupon they told me that they had heard I was going to experiment upon cake-making, and they would like to watch the proceedings and see how the cake turned out. Also they said they would help eat it, if at all eatable!

Thanking them for their interest and telling them to go home and bake their own cake, I started the task. I was interrupted once more by the hurried entrance of Captain T. M. Tolman of the First Infantry, who said the returning troops were reported as being but a few miles out, and as my husband was with them, he asked me if I would like to ride out and meet the troops. Of course I accepted his invitation, so I consigned the cake to the tender mercies of Kennedy, the cook, and made ready for my ride.

In the meantime my horse, Dandy, which Lieutenant Baldwin had bought from Captain Hale, was saddled and stood at the door, champing his bit and pawing the ground nervously, for he knew something unusual was going on — his horse instinct told him that. We were up and away without escort or orderly, for the depleted forces of the garrison would not have allowed that. We had made an early start. The sun shone hot, but the trail was favorable and our surefooted animals made no missteps, although prairie dog holes were numerous.

---

[42] Kennedy was a discharged soldier who became the family servant before the birth of Juanita in 1867 and remained with the Baldwins through their tour of duty at Fort Keogh. In 1879 when the Baldwins left Keogh, Kennedy bought a ranch and remained in the vicinity of Miles City, Montana.

We had ridden about four miles without catching sight of the reported troops, and while wondering where they could be I exclaimed, "There they are!" Captain Tolman adjusted his field glasses — he had them almost constantly to his eyes all the way — and gazing at the distant moving objects for some moments, he at length exclaimed, with some excitement in his voice, "Those aren't troops; they're either Indians or horse thieves. We've got to get back to the post as fast as we can dig!"

We turned about and *dug*! By this time the figures had developed into plainly evident white men — renegades and horse thieves, with whom the country was then infested and who were a menace to travelers. They had discovered us, and were near enough to covet the two superb horses we rode.

Presently they began shooting at us, and we bent low over our saddles to escape their shots, which were sent rapidly and too well aimed to make me feel very comfortable. Not a shot struck us, however, and the captain responded with his revolver, never slacking rein, and warning me "not to faint or throw a fit," but to keep up my courage, as he had got to land me safely at the post or he never could look my husband in the eye again. All these warnings and assuring words, shouted in the course of our flight, were heeded.

We were making good headway and distancing our pursuers, when to my horror my saddle girth broke. I shouted to the captain, "What shall I do now?" He called back to let the saddle drop in the road, and for me to "ride a-straddle." This I did without pausing. We were riding against the wind, and in my frantic efforts to keep my skirts down, I was making a display of "nether extremities" which did not exactly please me. I cautioned my sweating and swearing captain, "Don't look at me," to which he responded, "Damn your legs! Never mind your legs. I've got to get you home!" The dear man did, and landed me in safety at my own door, more dead than alive. I was bedraggled and skinned, covered with blisters and heat, disheveled and ragged — but, praise God, safe!

The people at the fort saw us coming and from our rapid pace discerned that something out of the ordinary had occurred. They ran out to meet us — men, women and children, and I was helped into the house, where the sympathetic surgeon, Dr. Sabin, administered to my bruises and blisters, alternating his sympathetic expressions to me with sundry strong language to the well-meaning captain.

What became of my side-saddle I never knew. A party was at once sent out to scout the country but the saddle was not to be found. Doubtless it was appropriated by the renegades who chased us.

Index

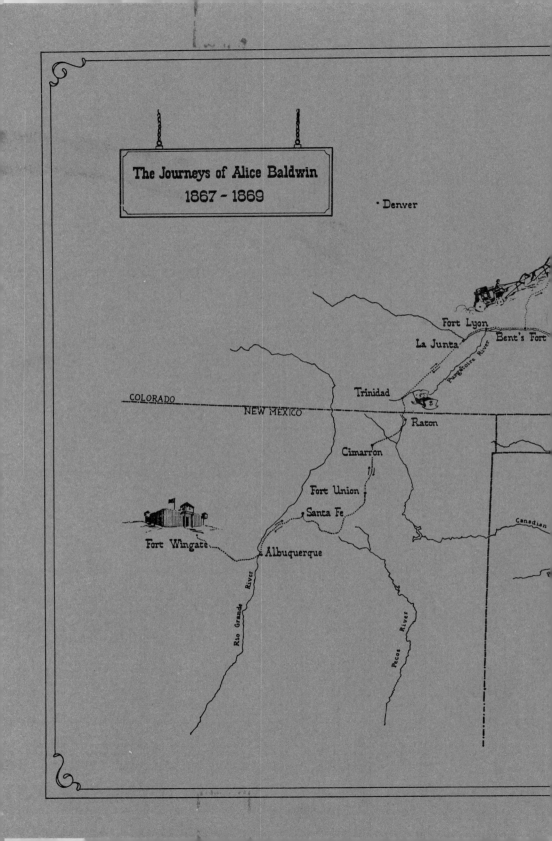

The Journeys of Alice Baldwin
1867 - 1869

· Denver

Fort Lyon

La Junta

Bent's Fort

Purgatoire River

COLORADO

NEW MEXICO

Trinidad

Raton

Cimarron

Fort Union

Santa Fe

Fort Wingate

Albuquerque

Rio Grande River

Pecos River

Canadian